Count Me In:

Resources for Making Music Inclusively with Children and Young People with Learning Difficulties

Adam Ockelford
Sophie Gray
Jon Cohen
Max Mai

Designed cover image: J. Griffin

First published 2023
by Routledge
4 Park Square, Milton Park, Abingdon, Oxon OX14 4RN

and by Routledge
605 Third Avenue, New York, NY 10158

Routledge is an imprint of the Taylor & Francis Group, an informa business

© 2023 Adam Ockelford, Sophie Gray, Jon Cohen and Max Mai

The right of Adam Ockelford, Sophie Gray, Jon Cohen and Max Mai to be identified as authors of this work has been asserted in accordance with sections 77 and 78 of the Copyright, Designs and Patents Act 1988.

All rights reserved. The purchase of this copyright material confers the right on the purchasing institution to photocopy pages which bear the photocopy icon and copyright line at the bottom of the page. No other parts of this book may be reprinted or reproduced or utilised in any form or by any electronic, mechanical, or other means, now known or hereafter invented, including photocopying and recording, or in any information storage or retrieval system, without permission in writing from the publishers.

Trademark notice: Product or corporate names may be trademarks or registered trademarks, and are used only for identification and explanation without intent to infringe.

British Library Cataloguing-in-Publication Data
A catalogue record for this book is available from the British Library

ISBN: 9781032215457 (hbk)
ISBN: 9781032215488 (pbk)
ISBN: 9781003268918 (ebk)

DOI: 10.4324/9781003268918

Printed in the UK by Severn, Gloucester on responsibly sourced paper

Publisher's note: This book has been prepared from camera-ready copy provided by the authors.

Adam Ockelford, https://en.wikipedia.org/wiki/Adam_Ockelford, is Professor of Music at the University of Roehampton in London. He has worked with children and young people across the spectrum of ability and need for the past four decades. He is the founder and chair of trustees of The Amber Trust, https://ambertrust.org, a UK-wide charity that supports blind and partially sighted children in their pursuit of music; founder and chair of trustees of Sounds of Intent Charity, https://www.soundsofintent.app, which promotes research and development into specialist and inclusive music education; and a trustee of Live Music Now, https://www.livemusicnow.org.uk, which uses music to enhance the lives of those experiencing social disadvantage.

Sophie Gray is Head of Inclusion at the Services for Education Music Service in Birmingham. She has over 20 years of experience in the field of music education, primarily in special schools, with particular expertise in working with children and young people with profound and multiple learning difficulties. She was among the first to undertake the Postgraduate Certificate in Special Musical Abilities and Needs in 2014 and now lectures on the course offered by the University of Roehampton.

Jon Cohen, https://www.joncohenmusic.co.uk, is an award-winning UK-based record producer and arranger. Working with artists across genres from classical to mainstream, Jon has an international reputation for delivering high quality commercial recordings, with fifteen No.1 classical/crossover albums, a winner of the Classical Brits album of the year, and sales of over 3.5 million albums. For the past few years, he has collaborated with Adam on a range of innovative projects, producing high-quality music specially designed for learners with special musical abilities or needs, including learning difficulties, deafness and visual impairment. For example, https://littleamber.ambertrust.org and https://www.soundaboutfamily.org.uk/soundabout-music-tracks/.

Max Mai, https://max-interactive.com, has over twenty years of experience of programming and web design for a range of prestigious commerical clients. His son, Mika, https://mika-mai.de, is a multitalented instrumentalist, despite being visually impaired and on the autism spectrum. Max and Adam have collaborated on a number of projects, including the production websites for The Amber Trust (for example, https://soundtouch.ambertrust.org) and Sounds of Intent Charity, https://www.soundsofintent.app.

Count Me In! is affectionately dedicated
to the memory of Pat Lloyd, gentle pioneer
in specialist music provision for children
and young people with differences
and disabilities.

Contents

Introduction 1

Autumn Elegy 14

Winter Lament 26

Spring Serenade 39

Summer Jig 53

Water Blues 67

Rainbow Rag 79

Urban Rap 93

Farm Reggae 105

Bollywood Party Dance 117

Spy Soundtrack 131

Olympic Harmony 143

Computer Chip Rock 155

Acknowledgements

We are grateful for the support of:

The National Foundation for Youth Music
Sounds of Intent Charity

The University of Roehampton
Services for Education, Birmingham

The teachers from the Services for Education, Birmingham and Solihull Music Service, and the school staff involved in the 'Inspiring Sounds' Project, funded by Youth Music.

The children, young people, their teachers and the musicians who worked with them on trialling the resources and who gave valuable feedback, particularly Carrie-Ann Plant and Sarah Hartland from The Bridge School in Sutton Coldfield, Martin Goodwin from Mary Elliot School in Walsall, and Aimee Warburton from Three Ways School in Bath, who worked with two musicians from Live Music Now, Bea Hubble and Chris Webb on an extended *Count Me In!* project, and Beth Pickard who evaluated it.

Evangelos Himonides for permission to use the photographs on pp. 38, 78 and 130.

Kathryn Puffet for her specialist copy-editing.

Clare Ashworth, Molly Kavanagh and the publications team at Routledge.

Introduction

Welcome to *Count Me In!* – a fully inclusive resource for making music with groups of children, young people and adults, whatever their abilities and needs. There are 12 pieces of music, each with sets of resources that will enable everyone to join in, including those with moderate, severe or profound learning difficulties, learners with sensory or physical impairments, children and young people who are on the autism spectrum and those functioning 'neurotypically' too. The materials are suitable for pupils and students attending special or mainstream schools or colleges, or for those participating in community performing arts groups. Whatever the setting, it is important for teachers, therapists, carers, parents and helpers to join in sessions too: **everyone is musical**.

There is no need to be able to read music to use *Count Me In!* as there are graphics explaining what is needed, and these are linked to downloadable audio files. However, there are also scores for specialist music teachers and visiting musicians who would like to use them, and simplified notation for participants (adults and children) whose musical literacy is at a less advanced stage. The *Count Me In!* resources can be used as the basis for classroom activities, potentially as part of wider topic-based learning, or they can provide the structure for performances, whether live, videoed or in a blended format.

Sounds of Intent

Count Me In! is based on the thinking developed in the Sounds of Intent project, which derives from the philosophy that difference and disability should be no barrier to musical engagement. Indeed, even people with severe learning difficulties, who may well find language and everyday understanding a challenge, can nevertheless have advanced musical skills. More information about Sounds of Intent is to be found at www.soundsofintent.app.[1]

At the heart of Sounds of Intent is an inclusive framework of musical development, which identifies six potential levels of engagement with music, from a stage before hearing gets going (typically, three months before birth) to a mature appreciation of music as a cultural artefact, capable of conveying an emotional narrative in sound, which typically occurs in the teenage years.

---

[1] Key publications setting out the principles of Sounds of Intent include '"Sounds of Intent": mapping musical behaviour and development in children and young people with complex needs' (2009) by Graham Welch, Adam Ockelford, Fern-Chantele Carter, Sally-Anne Zimmermann and Evangelos Himonides, in *Psychology of Music*, Vol. 37, No. 3, pp. 348–370; and 'Sounds of Intent: interactive software to assess the musical development of children and young people with complex needs' (2011) by Angela Vogiatzoglou, Adam Ockelford, Graham Welch and Evangelos Himonides, in *Music and Medicine*, Vol. 3, No. 3, pp. 189–195.

Level	Name	Description	Age of 'neurotypical' occurrence	Associated level of disability
1	learning to hear	before hearing gets going	prior to three months before birth	coma or vegetative state; the most profound learning difficulties
2	sounds interesting	sound is heard or made as a purely sensory experience	from three months before birth to around nine months	profound learning difficulties
3	copy me copy you	recognising simple patterns: anticipating and copying	from around nine months to around 15 months	severe or profound learning difficulties; may include autism
4	bits of pieces	hearing and creating groups of sounds as meaningful units of musical information, such as ringtones, motifs and riffs	from around 15 months to around 33 months	moderate or severe learning difficulties; may include autism
5	whole songs	intuitively understanding simple musical structures; singing short songs in time and in tune; playing relatively simple pieces	from around 33 months onwards	moderate or severe learning difficulties; may include autism
6	the wider world of music	appreciating music in a mature way as a language of the emotions; performing persuasively within a familiar culture, potentially at an advanced level	in the teenage years	moderate or severe learning difficulties; may include autism

Figure 1 The six levels of the Sounds of Intent framework.

In addition to these six levels, Sounds of Intent identifies three different ways in which people engage with music, called 'domains'. These are 'reactive', 'proactive' and 'interactive', and are colour-coded as follows:

Domain	Abbreviation	Description
reactive	R	listening and responding to sounds and music
proactive	P	making sounds, singing and playing alone
interactive	I	making sounds and music with other people

Figure 2 The three domains of the Sounds of Intent framework.

Mapping these three domains onto the six levels yields eighteen 'headlines' of musical engagement. These can be represented as segments in concentric circles, as shown in Figure 3. The expanding circles are intended as a metaphor for musical growth, moving from individuals with little or no awareness of themselves at the centre to sophisticated cultural participants in the outer ring.

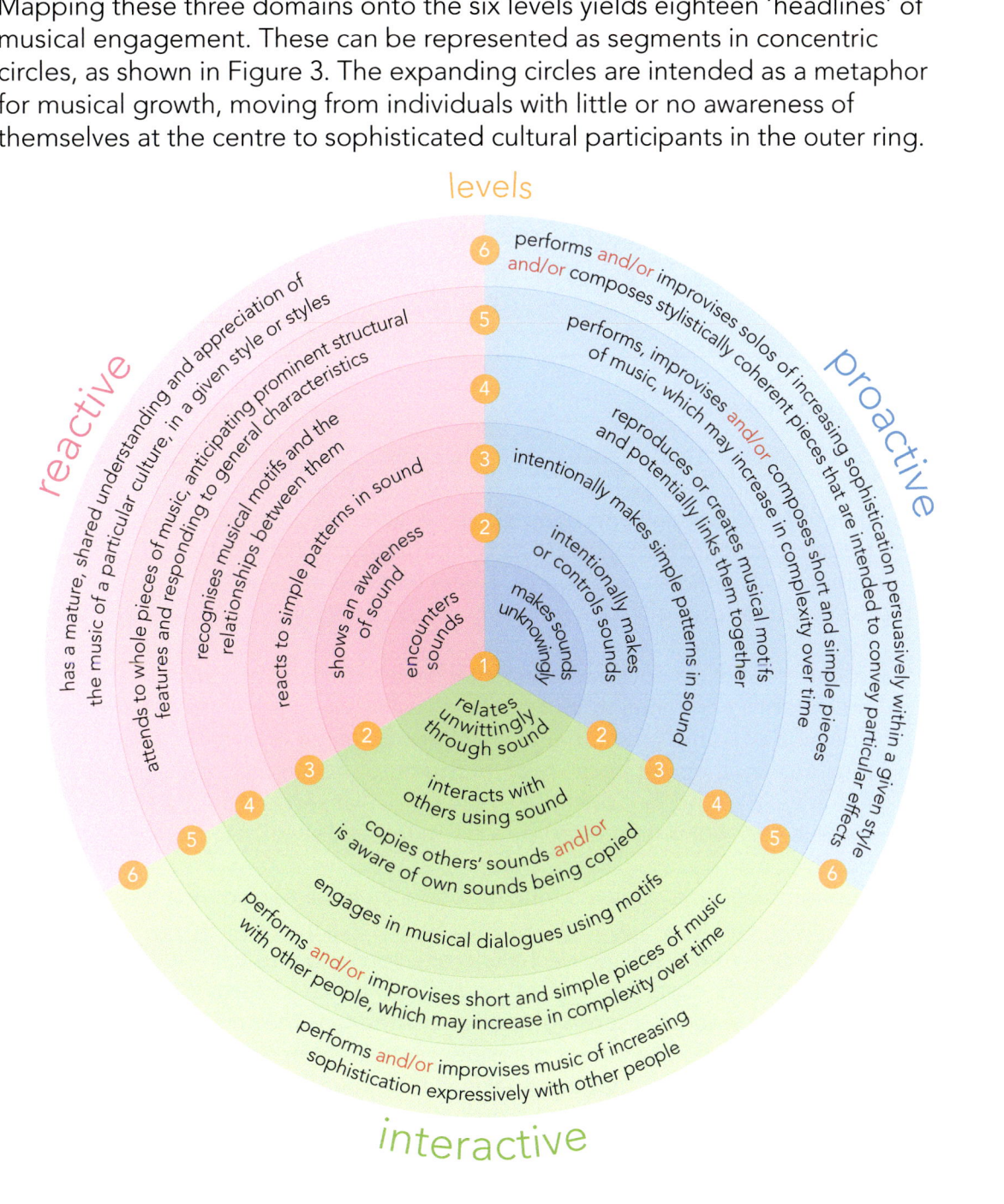

Figure 3 The Sounds of Intent framework of musical development.

Sounds of Intent levels should not be thought of as 'stages', in which one set of abilities replaces another. Rather, each level builds on those that precede as people's capacity to engage with music develops as they grow up and mature. This means that Sounds of Intent offers a bottom-up, 'can-do' account of musical engagement, that views all levels of ability positively – the opposite of a medical model that works 'top-down' and defines people by their deficits.

Labelling levels of musical engagement

Four of the Sounds of Intent levels are used in *Count Me In!* They are given the following, colour-coded labels to help make them easy to remember:

Level 2	Sound-makers
Level 3	Pattern-makers
Level 4	Motif-makers
Level 5	Music-makers

Sound-makers

'Sound-makers' experience music in a sensory way. It is likely that their capacity to engage with sound will still be developing, and that they will have an emerging ability to perceive an increasing range of sounds, to make sounds deliberately and consciously to interact with others using sound. These forms of engagement may well occur as part of wider, multisensory experiences.

Sound-makers do not yet consistently have a sense of pattern, predictability or imitation. But they may well have preferences for one type of sound or another and prefer one genre or piece of music to another, not because of its structure or meaning as a narrative in sound, but because of the particular sensory nature of the auditory world generated by a given musical style.

Sound-makers may well respond emotionally to certain sounds that they hear, and they may make sounds to express their feelings, vocally or through striking or shaking or scratching musical instruments or everyday objects. Sound may be an important factor too in their emerging sense of 'self' and 'other', as they make sounds in an effort to attract other people's attention and respond in turn to the sounds that they make. Hence sound may well be an indispensable element in the 'intensive interactions'[2] that often characterise the approach that teachers and carers adopt in seeking to engage with those who have profound and multiple learning difficulties.

---

[2] See *The Intensive Interaction Handbook* (2018) edited by Dave Hewett, published by Sage; and *Approaches to Communication through Music* (2002) by Margaret Corke, published by Routledge.

Pattern-makers

'Pattern-makers' are able to recognise some of the simple, moment-to-moment patterns created through repetition or regular change of which all music ultimately consists. The ability to perceive patterns in sound typically forms an important element in our understanding of the world, facilitating memory and fuelling anticipation, thereby enabling us mentally to reach out in time beyond the bubble of the present.[3] Similarly, the capacity to repeat sounds and to make a steady beat gives pattern-makers control over the present and enables them to plan what they are going to do next. Most importantly, pattern-makers' capacity to imitate others and to be aware of people copying them can provide insights into how those around think and feel: the foundations of 'theory of mind' and empathy.[4]

Motif-makers

'Motif-makers' can recognise and create the main building blocks of music: short, rhythmic groups of notes – brief bursts of melody – that Western classical musicians call 'motifs', jazzers refer to as 'riffs' or 'licks', pop singers describe as 'hooks' and advertising executives term 'stings'. The idea of distinctive, replicable groups of notes ties in with Richard Dawkins' notion of 'memes' – discrete, transferable units of cultural information.[5] It is groups of notes that give pieces of music their unique identities: think of a song, and it will be a motif that comes to mind – the first six notes of *Happy Birthday to You*, for example. Motifs can be an essential element in brand identities too: recall McDonald's five-note sting 'Ba Da Ba Ba Ba', which is associated with the tag 'I'm loving it', for instance.

---

[3] For more information see Edmund Husserl's classic text *The Phenomenology of Internal Time-Consciousness*, written at the turn of the twentieth century and republished by Martinus Nijhoff in The Hague in 1964.

[4] For more information see 'Towards a developmental model of musical empathy using insights from children who are on the autism spectrum and have learning difficulties' by Adam Ockelford, in *Music and Empathy* (2017) edited by Elaine King and Caroline Waddington, and published by Routledge in the SEMPRE series of *Studies in the Psychology of Music*.

[5] The pioneer in the area of musical memes is Steven Jan, whose book, *The Memetics of Music: A Neo-Darwinian View of Musical Structure and Culture*, was published in 2007 by Routledge.

As young children's musical abilities evolve in the early years, it is groups of notes that are the first elements to be stored in long-term musical memory (before complete pieces of music come to be memorised), and as three- or four-year olds they typically learn to re-create, vary and invent their own motifs. Through musical experimentation and play, children also learn how to connect groups of notes (borrowed or invented) to form what music psychologists have called 'pot pourri' songs.[6] The link between language and music is particularly noticeable at this stage in children's development, and they may copy each other's motifs with words and play 'call and response' games with their friends and carers.

Music-makers

'Music-makers' can grasp songs and other short pieces of music as self-contained entities. They recognise and can anticipate the prominent structural features such as the choruses of songs (even without the words). They intuitively respond to the general characteristics of music, such as its 'mode' (for example, whether it's in a major key, with its typically happy connotations, or in a minor key, which tends to evoke sadness) and its 'groove' (the overall rhythmic feel of a piece).

Music-makers show a developing ability to play or sing in time and (where relevant) in tune. For instance, they may sing songs which faithfully follow the contour of the original melody (its ups and downs in pitch) but where the intervals (the distances between one note and the next) are only approximately reproduced.

Music-makers may well enjoy singing and playing with others, either producing the same part as someone else or, increasingly, able to hold their own when others do something different. They may be able to improvise solos or work with other people to create new pieces of music too.

---

[6] A term first used by Helmut Moog in his book *The Musical Experiences of the Pre-school Child*, published in English in 1976 by Schott.

Since each of these different ways of engaging with music does not supersede those that come before, but incorporates them into a further stage of development, pattern-makers will always be sound-makers too, motif-makers will necessarily be pattern-makers and sound-makers as well, and music-makers, by definition, will also be sound-makers, pattern-makers and motif-makers. This becomes apparent when young people who are music-makers within their own culture are exposed to genres or instruments that are unfamiliar. Consider, for example, a group of children discovering the instruments of a gamelan for the first time.

Figure 4 The metallophones, gongs and drums used in gamelan, the traditional ensemble music of Bali and Java in Indonesia.

Without a conscious thought, the sound-maker latent within all of them is likely to surface immediately, as they explore the sensory nature of the instruments with their hands and listen attentively to the ringing sounds that the gongs make when they are struck. Beyond this initial exploration, pattern-making may emerge as the children tap beats on the drums or play short scales up and down the bars of the metallophones. These simple patterns will likely evolve into short bursts of melody – motifs – that may be repeated, copied and developed by others. Finally, with the guidance of a musician, these three elements may be consolidated in the creation of complete pieces, and the young people may revert to being fully fledged music-makers once more.

Learning to make sense of music

People in developed countries in particular are used to thinking about music primarily as an advanced form of art that is created by the few and consumed by the many. There is an enduring folk belief that musicians are born and not made, thanks to a fortunate genetic endowment.[7] Even in the scientific community, writers use the word 'gift' in speaking about musical potential,[8] and, in many psychological studies, a distinction is drawn between so-called 'musicians' and 'non-musicians'. But such a binary distinction makes no sense in anthropological terms. What would have been the evolutionary advantage to the developing human race of having an area of endeavour to which only a tiny minority were party?

As we have seen, the Sounds of Intent framework suggests that we are all musical. For sure, some people have the potential and the propensity to develop musical abilities more fully than others, and performances of music as art typically demand a high degree of physical and cognitive skills and a sophisticated level of affective understanding that only advanced singers and players have acquired. But if those listening to them were unable to appreciate the music they produced – albeit intuitively – then performances, in person, online, live or recorded, would not attract audiences, and we can reasonably suppose that music as an art form would never have got off the ground.

There is a general recognition that to become an expert performing musician takes thousands of hours of practice through childhood and adolescence.[9] But how do children develop the capacity to engage with music as listeners? That is, how do they move from the level of merely perceiving sound to processing sonic patterns; how do they learn to recognise motifs and, beyond that, acquire the ability to grasp whole pieces as they unfold over time? As Figure 1 shows, these skills typically evolve in the early years, long before formal music education begins. As the old adage has it, an understanding of music seems to be 'caught not taught'. How does this occur?

---

[7] See https://www.quora.com/Do-people-choose-to-be-musicians-or-are-they-born-with-talent.
[8] See a number of the chapters in Gary McPherson's edited book *Musical Prodigies: Interpretations from Psychology, Education, Musicology & Ethnomusicology* (2016), published by Oxford University Press.
[9] For a popular account of the relationship between practice and mastery of a complex skill, see Malcolm Gladwell's book *Outliers: The Story of Success*, published in 2008 by Penguin Books. For research suggesting that 'effortful practice is a determinant of musical achievement', see 'The role of practice in the development of performing musicians', by John Sloboda, Jane Davidson, Michael Howe and Derek Moore (1996), in the *British Journal of Psychology*, Vol. 87, No. 2, pp. 287–309.

While parents intuitively simplify things for their children, singing them lullabies and nursery rhymes, and copying their babbling sounds through 'parentese',[10] most of the music to which children are exposed in everyday life – and they experience a great deal of music during their waking hours[11] – is designed by adults for listeners, young and old, who are already competent at Sounds of Intent Level 5 or beyond. What are young, still-developing musical ears likely to make of it all? As the example of the gamelan given above suggests, the intrinsically multilayered design of music means that pieces have qualities and features that can potentially appeal to sound-makers, pattern-makers, motif-makers and music-makers at the same time, offering a meaningful musical experience at all levels at once. It seems that the auditory systems of young, 'typically-developing' human brains can extract aspects of music automatically at levels that match their individual functional capacities. Moreover, this ability appears to develop merely through exposure. For example, consider a piece of Western classical music – 'Dido's Lament' from Henry Purcell's opera *Dido and Aeneas*, as sung by Emma Kirkby.[12]

According to the Sounds of Intent framework and research undertaken in the field of 'applied musicology' (which indicates that we can get a sense of what is happening in the 'black box' of the musical mind by the responses that children make to auditory stimuli),[13] we can reasonably expect scenarios such as the following. Seven-month-old Sam experiences a flow of changing sounds as he listens to the lament, while Mattie, 14 months old, detects simple patterns such as the regular beat and the rising and falling patterns of pitch. Amrit, at two years and four months, attends to repeating motifs, such as those to which the words 'remember me' are set, while Xiu, soon to turn five, intuitively grasps the structure of the piece as a whole, with its repeats and the symmetry of the instrumental opening and closing sections.

---

[10] The vocal interactions between babies and their parents are framed as early, interactive music-making by Stephen Malloch and Colwyn Trevarthen in their book *Communicative Musicality: Exploring the Basis of Human Companionship*, published in 2008 by Oxford University Press.

[11] See, for example, Alex Lamont's study of 2006, 'Toddlers' musical worlds: musical engagement in 3.5 year olds', in the *Proceedings of the 9th International Conference on Music Perception and Cognition (ICMPC9)*, edited by Mario Baroni, Anna Rita Addessi, Roberto Caterina and Marco Costa.

[12] See https://www.youtube.com/watch?v=H3wAarmPYKU.

[13] A topic discussed in some detail in Chapter 3 of *Applied Musicology: Using Zygonic Theory to Inform Music Education, Therapy, and Psychology Research* by Adam Ockelford, published by Oxford University Press in 2013.

increasing sophistication of engagement

music-maker — Xiu — grasps the structure of the piece as a whole — 56 months

sound-maker — Sam — experiences a flow of changing sounds — 7 months

Emma Kirkby

motif-maker — Amrit — recognises key motifs — 28 months

pattern-maker — Mattie — detects simple patterns — 14 months

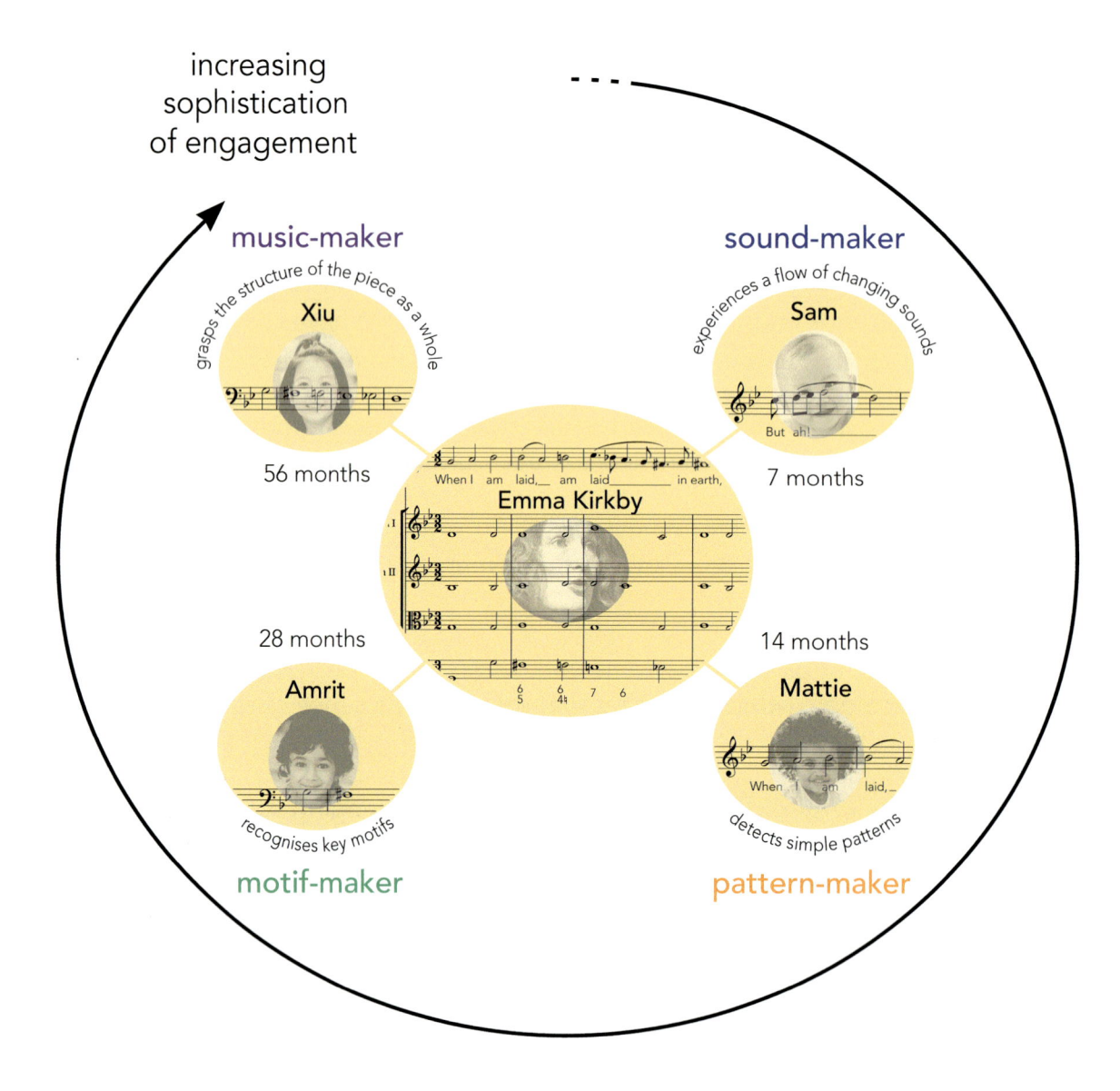

Figure 5 Modelling what young children at different music-developmental stages may hear when they are exposed to a piece of traditional Western classical music.

In summary, for children in the early years who are developing 'neurotypically', it seems that mere exposure to music of their culture over three or four years is sufficient for them intuitively to grasp the way it is structured and its emotional import, and so unthinkingly to extract meaning from what they hear. Given the complexity of this task, the fact that it occurs without the need for formal music tuition is an extraordinary achievement of the young human brain.

Musical development in children with learning difficulties

But what of those with learning difficulties? Sounds of Intent research suggests that they tread the same music-developmental path as their neurotypical peers, though usually at a different rate. For example, the musical abilities of a small number of children with learning difficulties who are on the autism spectrum may develop precociously, not only in terms of advanced listening skills, but also in relation to exceptional expertise in performance, while they are still very young.[14] The musical development of the majority of those with cognitive impairments, though, is slower than average, with milestones being reached later in childhood than is typically the case and, particularly for those with profound disabilities, most not being achieved.

Why should this be the case? It appears that the incidental musical learning that usually features in the early years may not occur in profoundly disabled children, and that this may exacerbate the music-developmental delay that their global learning difficulties would in any case incur. The evidence for this comes from a number of studies undertaken in a range of contexts, which show that targeted musical activities that match (or slightly exceed) the music-developmental levels of those with profound and multiple disabilities can expedite their progress.[15] That is to say, when the implicit learning they don't experience is replaced with explicit tuition – through the provision of 'enabling environments' that include appropriate resources and staff who are trained to use them to interact empathetically through sound – it may be that even those with profound cognitive impairments can acquire a higher level of musical skill than their global level of development would initially suggest was probable.

The findings of this research have underpinned the development of several sets of resources, based on the thinking set out in the Sounds of Intent framework. These offer teachers, teaching assistants, therapists, parents and carers ideas for musical activities that they can undertake with children and young people with severe, or profound and multiple learning difficulties, targeted at individuals' music-developmental levels.[16] However, many children and young people with learning difficulties experience music in groups whose members are functioning

---

[14] Accounts of the exceptional musicality of some young autistic children are to be found in Adam Ockelford's book *Music, Language and Autism: Exceptional Strategies for Exceptional Minds*, published by Jessica Kingsley in 2013.

[15] See, for example, '*Sounds of Intent*, Phase 2: approaches to the quantification of music-developmental data pertaining to children with complex needs', by Adam Ockelford, Graham Welch, Lamorna Jewell-Gore, Evangeline Cheng, Angela Vogiatzoglou and Evangelos Himonides, published in 2011 in the *European Journal of Special Needs Education*, Vol. 26, No. 2, pp. 177–199.

[16] Most of these are freely available online. See, for instance, https://amberplus.ambertrust.org and https://www.soundaboutfamily.org.uk.

on a range of music-developmental levels, whether in their regular class music sessions at school, through workshops organised by visiting musicians or when participating in community music events. Moreover, the rise of inclusive choirs[17] and ensembles such as the National Open Youth Orchestra,[18] which welcome both disabled and non-disabled performers, has meant that the range of abilities within music-making groups can be very wide indeed. What is needed, therefore, are resources that utilise the multilayered nature of music – with its sounds, patterns, motifs and more extensive structures – to offer all participants in a group ways of engaging with a given piece that suit them, while fitting together coherently as a whole; that is, through 'differentiation' – the process through which learning materials and teaching styles are modified to suit individuals' needs, abilities and preferences. This is what *Count Me In!* aims to achieve.

Count Me In!

Count Me In! comprises 12 fully inclusive musical activities, each of which 'deconstructs' a song (or, in one case, an instrumental piece) into elements that are suitable for sound-makers, pattern-makers, motif-makers and music-makers. The idea is that participants practise their parts individually (with whatever level of support is required), before using what they have learnt to contribute to a group. It is important that everyone involved – including teachers, teaching assistants, therapists, parents, carers – should regard themselves as an active participant in what is going on and make their own musical contribution. Sessions may be led by specialist musicians, perhaps visiting a school as part of a wider project or directing a community music group, but non-specialist teachers, carers and others can take the initiative too; there is no need to be able to read music to make use of *Count Me In!*

The activities aim to cover a wide range of styles rooted in different musical cultures. Each focuses on a topic with contemporary relevance, and the sentiments expressed are appropriate for people of all ages.[19]

---

[17] See, for example, https://www.soundabout.org.uk/soundabout-inclusive-choir/ and https://include.org/the-include-choir/.

[18] https://noyo.org.uk.

[19] The issue of the age-appropriateness of the musical resources available to those working with adolescents and adults with learning difficulties has been the subject of debate for some time. See, for example, 'Music in the education of children with severe or profound learning difficulties: issues in current UK provision, a new conceptual framework, and proposals for research' by Adam Ockelford, published in 2000 in *Psychology of Music*, Vol. 28, No. 2, pp. 197–217.

1. Autumn Elegy
2. Winter Lament
3. Spring Serenade
4. Summer Jig
5. Water Blues
6. Rainbow Rag
7. Urban Rap
8. Farm Reggae
9. Bollywood Party Dance
10. Spy Soundtrack
11. Olympic Harmony
12. Computer Chip Rock

Each activity is set out in a similar way. The first two pages comprise an introduction, which sets the context for the piece, followed by a list of the musical resources required in terms of instruments, music technology and everyday objects that make sounds. These should be regarded as indicative rather than prescriptive. Additional items that can be used to realise the multisensory potential of the activities, are also suggested. Strategies for introducing the materials are set out, and links to other areas of experience and learning are highlighted. These may be particularly helpful for those planning and delivering curricula in schools and colleges.

Four sections follow, devoted respectively to sound-makers, pattern-makers, motif-makers and music-makers. For ease of use, a consistent colour-coding scheme is used throughout: sound-makers' materials are shown in blue, pattern-makers' are in green, motif-makers' in orange and music-makers' in purple. Ideas for participation are illustrated using graphics. Simplified music notation is also used, showing rhythms with notes of different lengths and letters for pitch. There are conventional scores for specialist music teachers and visiting musicians. Pages with the photocopiable icon and copyright line can be copied for ease of use, provided a *Count Me In!* book has been purchased legitimately. Throughout the resource pages, there are links to the *Count Me In!* website www.soundsofintent.app/count-me-in, which has a substantial library of down-loadable digital audio files.

The materials are designed to be used flexibly, in the classroom and beyond, with groups of different sizes and ranges of ability. The 'backing tracks' (with and without words) will ensure musical coherence, whatever contributions participants make; if people choose not to play or sing, or are absent, the music will continue. Above all, *Count Me In!* should be regarded not as an end in itself, but as a starting point for promoting individuals' self-expression and creativity. To this end, periods of silence are built into the backing tracks to encourage spontaneous contributions. Using the principles that are set out, teachers and visiting musicians will be able to produce new pieces – ideally using ideas generated by the participants themselves.

Introduction

Autumn Elegy reflects on four features of the season, with a verse devoted to each: leaves falling from the trees, swallows preparing to migrate, hedgehogs readying themselves for hibernation and fireworks lighting up the night sky. The song is in the style of a jazz waltz, characterised by its syncopated rhythm. A famous example is Miles Davis's version of *Someday my Prince Will Come.*

Each verse has parts for sound-makers, pattern-makers, motif-makers and music-makers. This means that all participants, irrespective of their level of musical development, can play or sing together. Between verses there are sections in which everyone can contribute using pre-recorded sounds of leaves swirling in the breeze, swallows singing, hedgehogs snuffling and snoring, and fireworks going off.

Musical resources required

Choose from the following, according to participants' abilities, preferences and needs:

Sound-Makers

- Frame drum(s)
- A tray of dry leaves
- Control of digitally recorded scratching sounds and the sounds of rustling leaves through
    - gesture recognition technology (tablets/beams)
    - eye gaze technology
    - switch(es)

    that are loaded with sound files from https://www.soundsofintent.app/count-me-in
- Microphone(s) and amplifier(s) with effects unit(s)

Pattern-Makers

- Drum(s), wood block(s), tambourine(s)
- Individually recorded sounds using switch(es), tablet(s) or computer keyboard(s) that are loaded with sound files of single notes on unpitched percussion instruments, or of swallow chirps from https://www.soundsofintent.app/count-me-in

Motif-Makers

- Cabasa(s)
- Keyboard(s), recorder(s), other wind instruments
- Tablet(s) or computer keyboard(s) loaded with hedgehog sounds from https://www.soundsofintent.app/count-me-in
- Microphone(s) and amplifier(s) with effects unit(s)

Music-Makers

- Keyboard(s), recorder(s) and/or other wind instrument(s), tablet(s)
- Guitar(s), ukulele(s), bass guitar(s)
- Computer(s) and/or tablet(s) with software to create a soundscape using digital recordings of fireworks downloaded from https://www.soundsofintent.app/count-me-in
- Microphone(s) and amplifier(s)

Additional items

Participants can experience *Autumn Elegy* in a multisensory way, with trays of dry leaves to feel and scrunch, for example, with videos of swallows gathering before they migrate, of hedgehogs making their nests and of firework displays, and with the smells of jacket potatoes and sausages.

Strategies

Make time to listen to *Autumn Elegy* a few times over a number of days before encouraging participants to engage actively with the music. This may help them become familiar with the sounds, patterns, motifs, melodies and harmonies that are used. Remember that, in musical development – and in aural traditions – listening precedes active participation.

Individual parts can be practised one-to-one, and then in pairs or small groups, before you try to bring the whole texture together.

With each verse, using the backing track, start by encouraging sound-makers to join in, then pattern-makers and motif-makers before music-makers come in with the main melody. The arrangements are suitable for groups of different sizes. If some participants are not present or choose not to play or sing, the backing track will hold things together.

Links to other areas of experience and learning

In schools and colleges, *Autumn Elegy* has potential links to other curricular areas, such as science (the seasons and, perhaps, why regular changes in the weather occur and the impact of global warming) and geography (how autumn varies from one continent to another, the harvesting of food, and the rituals and customs associated with autumn in different cultures).

Autum

Sound-Makers

During each verse

Some participants may make scratching sounds on a frame drum from time to time.

frame drum

Or they make similar sounds using gesture recognition technology such as that available on tablets and using beams,

beam   **tablet**

or by using switches or eye gaze technology.

switch   **eye gaze**

Some participants may like to join in by making their own vocal sounds, which can be enhanced using an amplifier and effects unit if there is one available.

mic

Verse 1
It's autumn time, and now the leaves
Are swirling in the breeze.
They're falling, falling, falling, falling,
Falling from the trees.

Verse 2
It's autumn time, and now the swallows
Swoop as they fly.
They're singing, singing, singing, singing,
Singing goodbye.

Verse 3
It's autumn time, and now the hedgehogs
Curl up in their nests.
They're sleeping, sleeping, sleeping, sleeping,
Sleeping sound, at rest.

Verse 4
It's autumn time, and now it's dark
The fireworks catch my eye.
They're whistling, fizzing, hissing, sizzling,
Whizzing up high.

They're bursting, booming, popping, zooming,
Dropping from the sky.

Elegy

Sound-Makers

After Verse 1

Sounds of leaves rustling

Some participants may like to rustle leaves themselves, perhaps provided in a tray placed under their hands or feet. Any sounds could be enhanced using a microphone and amplifier.

Sounds of swallows singing

Others may prefer to join in with the sounds of rustling leaves using downloaded digital sounds, controlled with devices such as switches, beams, tablets and eye-gaze technology.

Sounds of hedgehogs grunting, snuffling and snoring

switch   eye gaze

beam   tablet

Sounds of different fireworks in a display

Copyright material from Ockelford, Gray, Cohen and Mai (2023), *Count Me In!*, Routledge

Autumn

Pattern-Makers

During each verse

Show participants how to join in with the slow, regular beat of the song on a drum or other non-pitched percussion instrument. For example:

bang — bang
drum

tap — tap
wood block

hit — hit
tambourine

Others may prefer to use downloaded percussive sounds triggered by using a switch or on a tablet.

switch — tablet

Verse 1
It's autumn time, and now the leaves
Are swirling in the breeze.
They're falling, falling, falling, falling,
Falling from the trees.

Verse 2
It's autumn time, and now the swallows
Swoop as they fly.
They're singing, singing, singing, singing,
Singing goodbye.

Verse 3
It's autumn time, and now the hedgehogs
Curl up in their nests.
They're sleeping, sleeping, sleeping, sleeping,
Sleeping sound, at rest.

Verse 4
It's autumn time, and now it's dark
The fireworks catch my eye.
They're whistling, fizzing, hissing, sizzling,
Whizzing up high.

They're bursting, booming, popping, zooming,
Dropping from the sky.

Copyright material from Ockelford, Gray, Cohen and Mai (2023), *Count Me In!*, Routledge

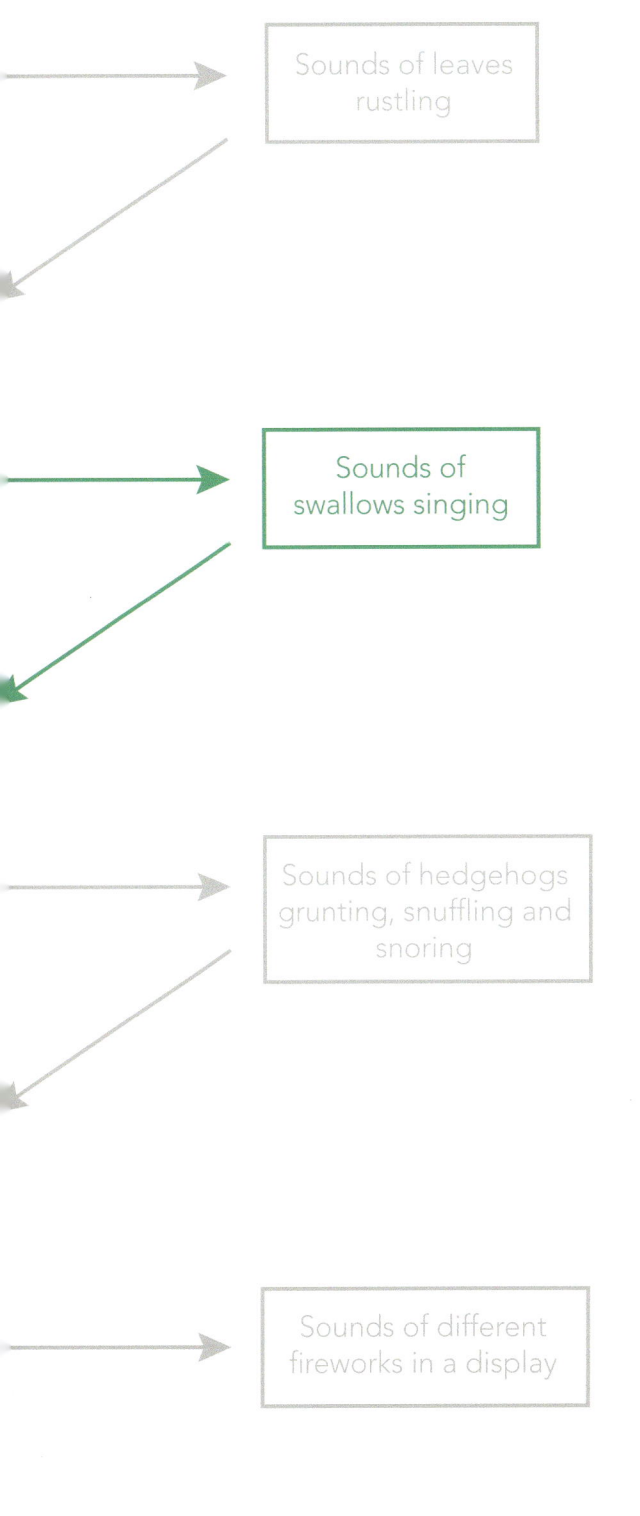

Elegy

Pattern-Makers

After Verse 2

Demonstrate how to make regular patterns of swallows singing by repeatedly pressing a switch, touchscreen or key on a computer keyboard, loaded with a single digital swallow chirp, at different speeds.

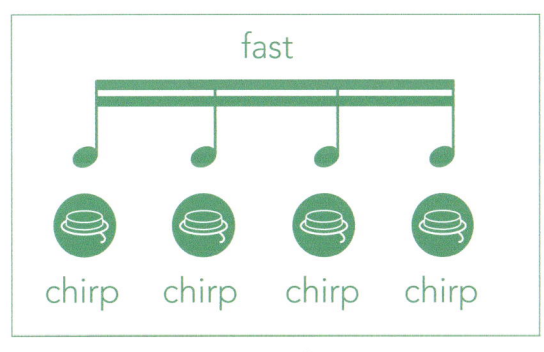

Sounds of leaves rustling

Sounds of swallows singing

Sounds of hedgehogs grunting, snuffling and snoring

Sounds of different fireworks in a display

fast

| chirp | chirp | chirp | chirp |

switch

medium

| chirp | chirp |

tablet

slow

| chirp | chirp |

computer keyboard

Copyright material from Ockelford, Gray, Cohen and Mai (2023), *Count Me In!*, Routledge

Autumn

Motif-Makers

During each verse

Encourage participants to join in with the jazz waltz rhythm on the cabasa. To keep in time, it may help to think of short groups of words. For example:

1	&	2	3	1	&	2	3
'rhy	- thm,		the	rhy	- thm,		the ...'

cabasa

A two-note melodic motif is repeated all the way through the piece. Listen for it in the introduction, and encourage participants to join in on a keyboard or a wind instrument such as the recorder, or on a tablet, or by humming or singing to 'lah' (using a microphone if wished).

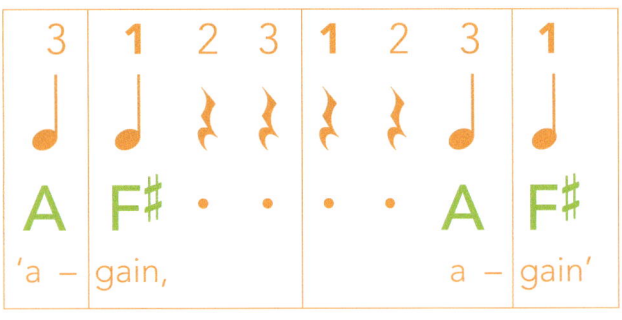

3	1	2	3	1	2	3	1
A	F#	.	.	.	.	A	F#
'a –	gain,					a –	gain'

keys recorder tablet mic

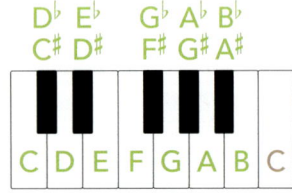

D♭ E♭   G♭ A♭ B♭
C# D#   F# G# A#

C D E F G A B C

Names of notes on a keyboard

Verse 1
It's autumn time, and now the leaves
Are swirling in the breeze.
They're falling, falling, falling, falling,
Falling from the trees.

Verse 2
It's autumn time, and now the swallows
Swoop as they fly.
They're singing, singing, singing, singing,
Singing goodbye.

Verse 3
It's autumn time, and now the hedgehogs
Curl up in their nests.
They're sleeping, sleeping, sleeping, sleeping,
Sleeping sound, at rest.

Verse 4
It's autumn time, and now it's dark
The fireworks catch my eye.
They're whistling, fizzing, hissing, sizzling,
Whizzing up high.

They're bursting, booming, popping, zooming,
Dropping from the sky.

Copyright material from Ockelford, Gray, Cohen and Mai (2023), *Count Me In!*, Routledge

Elegy

Motif-Makers

After Verse 3

Show participants how to connect different groups of hedgehog sounds – snuffling, grunting, snoring – together in different ways, choosing from digital collections of sounds triggered by buttons on computers or the screens of tablets or phones.

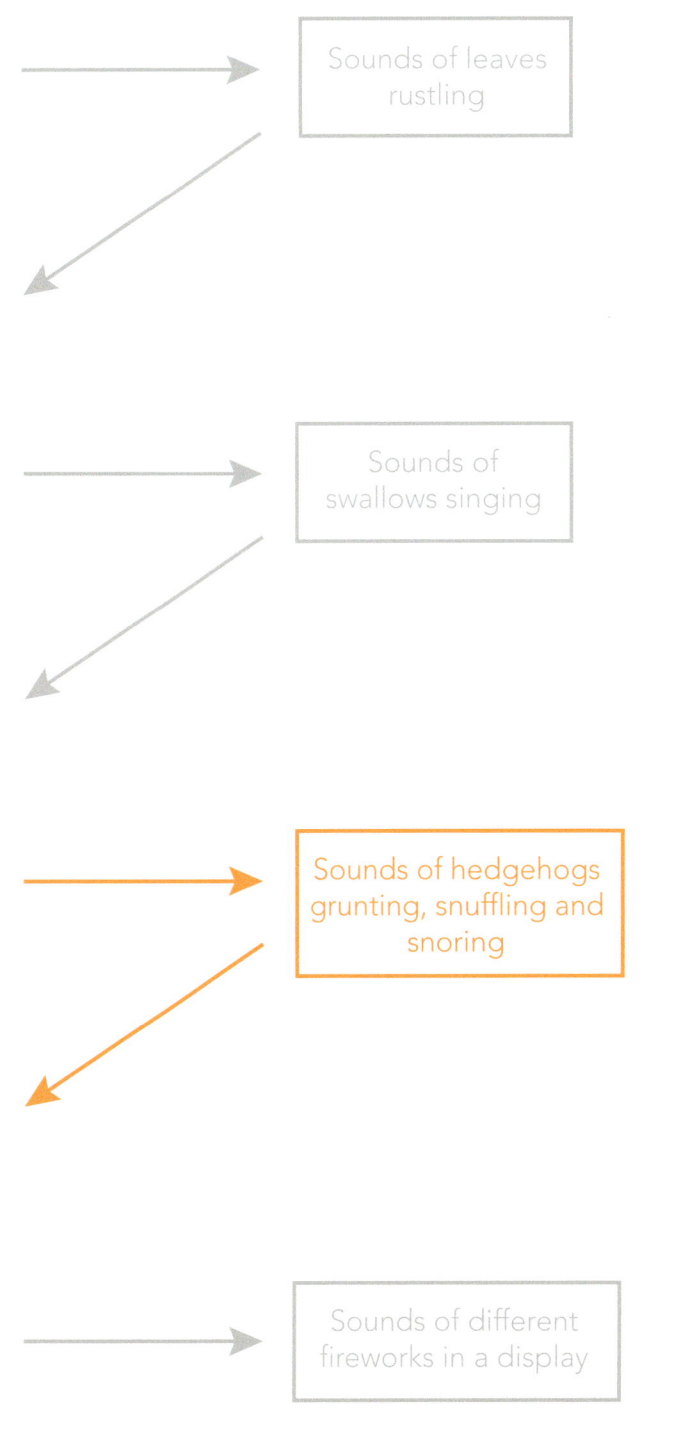

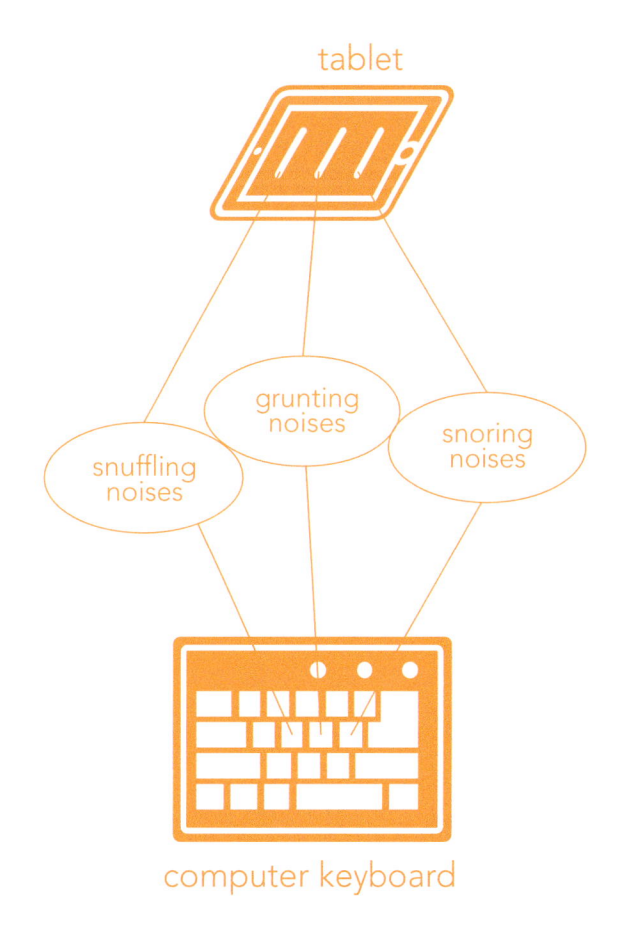

→ Sounds of leaves rustling

→ Sounds of swallows singing

→ **Sounds of hedgehogs grunting, snuffling and snoring**

→ Sounds of different fireworks in a display

tablet

snuffling noises — grunting noises — snoring noises

computer keyboard

Or some participants may like to try to reproduce the sounds vocally, using a microphone and effects unit, if one is available.

mic

Copyright material from Ockelford, Gray, Cohen and Mai (2023), *Count Me In!*, Routledge

Autumn

Verse 1
It's autumn time, and now the leaves
Are swirling in the breeze.
They're falling, falling, falling, falling,
Falling from the trees.

→ Sounds of leaves rustling

Verse 2
It's autumn time, and now the swallows
Swoop as they fly.
They're singing, singing, singing, singing,
Singing goodbye.

→ Sounds of swallows singing

Verse 3
It's autumn time, and now the hedgehogs
Curl up in their nests.
They're sleeping, sleeping, sleeping, sleeping,
Sleeping sound, at rest.

→ Sounds of hedgehogs grunting, snuffling and snoring

Verse 4
It's autumn time, and now it's dark
The fireworks catch my eye.
They're whistling, fizzing, hissing, sizzling,
Whizzing up high.

They're bursting, booming, popping, zooming,
Dropping from the sky.

→ Sounds of different fireworks in a display

Elegy

Music-Makers
During each verse

Some participants may be able to sing or play the tune on a melody instrument (such as a keyboard or recorder). Others may play the bass line on a keyboard or bass guitar. Play the chords on a keyboard, guitar or ukulele, using simpler versions (in bold, without the 7ths) if preferred.

- keys
- recorder
- bass
- guitar
- ukulele
- mic

Melody / Right hand

Additional tune	A	F#—F#	F#—G	A—A	A—A	B—A	A—B	A—F#	— ·		
Simple version	·	D— ·	D— ·	F#— ·	F#— ·	A— ·	E— ·	D— ·			
Full version	F#	D—D	D—E	F#—F#	F#—G	A—F#	E—F#	D— ·			

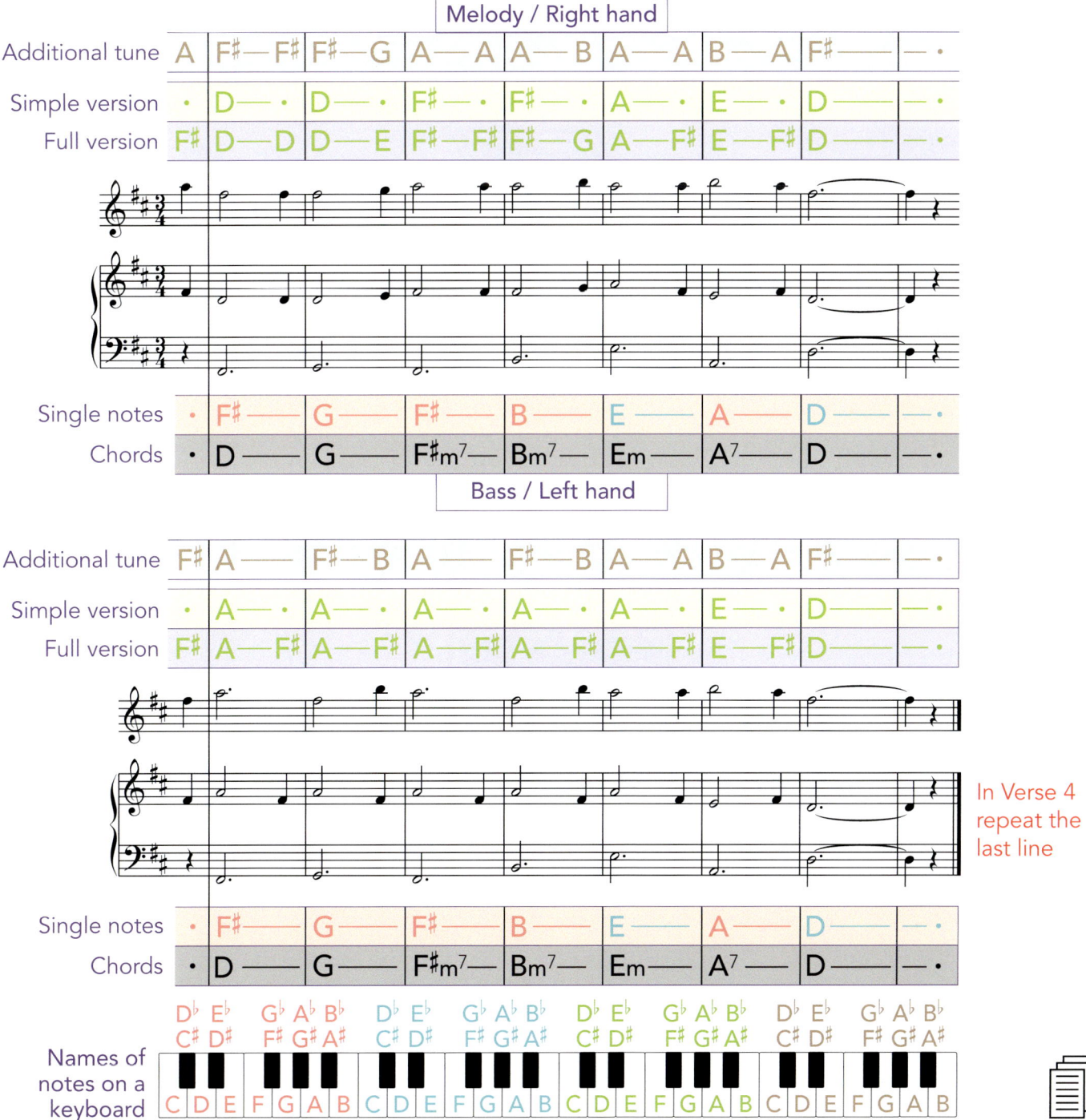

Bass / Left hand

Single notes	·	F#—	G—	F#—	B—	E—	A—	D— ·			
Chords	·	D—	G—	F#m⁷—	Bm⁷—	Em—	A⁷—	D— ·			

Additional tune	F#	A—	F#—B	A—	F#—B	A—A	B—A	F#—	— ·		
Simple version	·	A— ·	A— ·	A— ·	A— ·	A— ·	E— ·	D— ·			
Full version	F#	A—F#	A—F#	A—F#	A—F#	A—F#	E—F#	D— ·			

In Verse 4 repeat the last line

Single notes	·	F#—	G—	F#—	B—	E—	A—	D— ·			
Chords	·	D—	G—	F#m⁷—	Bm⁷—	Em—	A⁷—	D— ·			

Names of notes on a keyboard: C D E F G A B (repeated across keyboard), with black keys D♭/C#, E♭/D#, G♭/F#, A♭/G#, B♭/A#.

Copyright material from Ockelford, Gray, Cohen and Mai (2023), *Count Me In!*, Routledge

Music-Makers

After Verse 4

Before a performance of *Autumn Elegy*, create a short soundscape of digitally recorded firework sounds made by technological devices using an app such as GarageBand. Replay the montage of sounds after Verse 4.

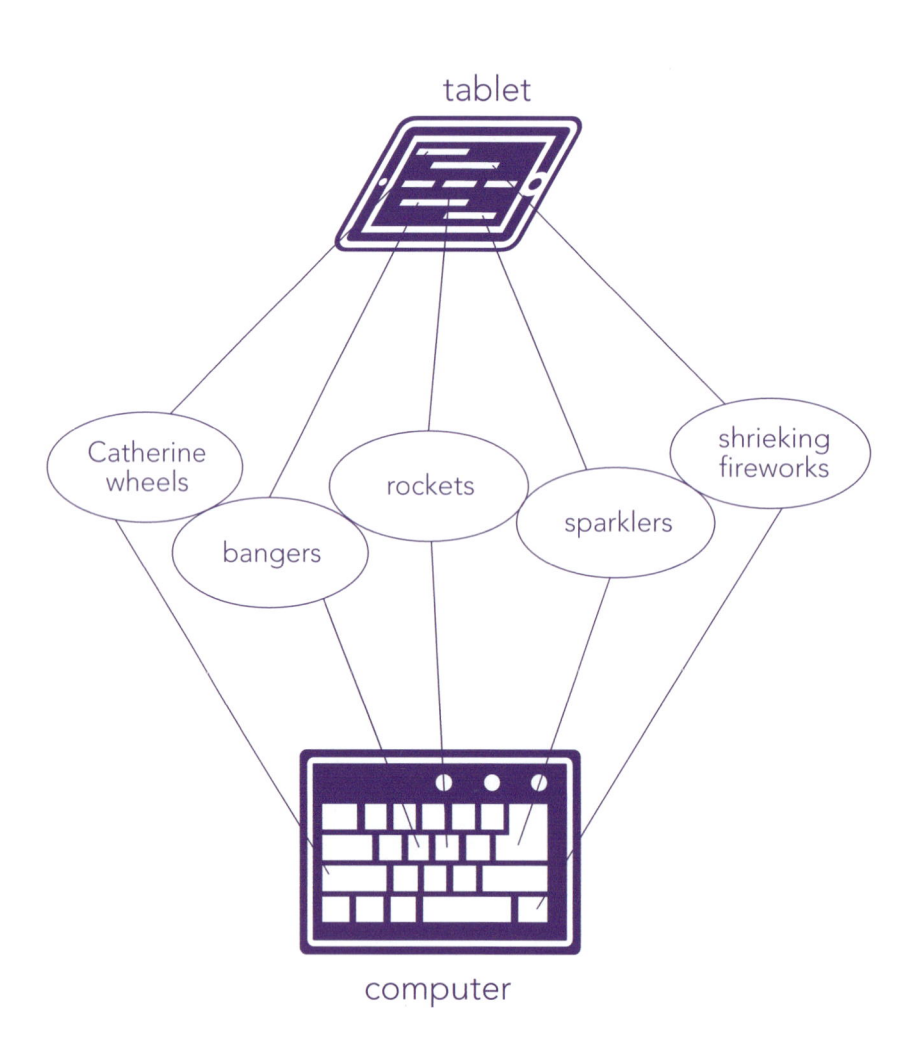

tablet

- Catherine wheels
- bangers
- rockets
- sparklers
- shrieking fireworks

computer

Elegy

Score for music teachers to use

Keyboard — DMaj7 GMaj7 F#m7 Bm7 Em11 A7 D

Optional melody instrument

Voice — DMaj7 GMaj7 F#m7 Bm7 Em11 A7 D

1. It's au – tumn time, and now the leaves are swirl – ing in the breeze.
2. It's au – tumn time, and now the swal – lows swoop___ as they fly.
3. It's au – tumn time, and now the hedge-hogs curl up in their nests.
4. It's au – tumn time, and now it's dark the fire – works catch my eye.

DMaj7 GMaj7 F#m7 Bm7 Em11 A7 D

1. They're fall – ing, fall – ing, fall – ing, fall – ing, fall – ing from the trees.
2. They're sing – ing, sing - ing, sing – ing, sing – ing, sing___ ing good–bye.
3. They're sleep–ing, sleep–ing, sleep – ing, sleep – ing, sleep – ing sound, at rest.
4. They're whist–ling, fizz – ing, hiss – ing, sizz – ling, whizz___ ing up high.
   They're burst–ing, boom-ing, pop – ping, zoom – ing, drop – ping from the sky.

In Verse 4 repeat the last line of music

Copyright material from Ockelford, Gray, Cohen and Mai (2023), *Count Me In!*, Routledge

Winte

Introduction

A lament is an expression of sadness. Musical laments feature in many different cultures across the globe. In Western classical music, perhaps the most celebrated example is 'Dido's Lament' from the end of Henry Purcell's late seventeenth century opera *Dido and Aeneas*, where Dido sings of her unbearable grief at the loss of Aeneas and dies of a broken heart.

Winter Lament starts sadly, but ends with a ray of hope, as birdsong reminds us that spring is on the way. Before that, the lament sets out different winter scenes in four short verses: rain and snow being blown into one's face by the north wind; puddles freezing and trapping leaves that have fallen from the trees; freezing rain and hail drumming on a windowpane; and the scrunch of footsteps on snow-packed ground. The mood is mournful, expressed through the use of the minor key, the repeated sounds of bells, the constant presence of deep sustained notes and an unrelenting, ponderous beat. In the fifth scene, although the world is grey, the fact that birds still sing as dawn breaks leaves us with a sense of hope, and the cold of the minor key is replaced with the warmth of the major.

The five verses of *Winter Lament* have parts for sound-makers, pattern-makers, motif-makers and music-makers. This means that everyone in a group, whatever their capacity to engage with music, can make sounds, sing and play together. After each verse there are improvised sections, intended for participants with varying musical abilities. The first two, which portray the wind blowing and leaves scrunching underfoot, are intended for sound-makers. The third and fourth sections, which depict hail drumming on a windowpane and the sound of someone walking on tightly-packed snow, are meant for pattern-makers. The fifth improvised section, comprising birds singing in the dawn chorus, is for motif-makers.

Musical resources required

Choose from the following, according to participants' abilities, preferences and needs:

Sound-Makers

- Chime bars, hand bells, tubular bells, glockenspiel(s), cymbal(s)
- Control of digitally recorded bell-like sounds, the sounds of wind and rain, and of leaves being scrunched, through
    - gesture recognition technology (tablets/beams)
    - eye gaze technology
    - switch(es)

  that are loaded with sound files from https://www.soundsofintent.app/count-me-in
- Microphone(s) and amplifier(s), potentially with loop pedal and effects

Pattern-Makers

- Large (bass) drum(s), cow bell(s), claves, cabasa(s), wood block(s)
- Pattern-making through individually recorded sounds of hailstones hitting a windowpane and footsteps in the snow using a switch or switches that are loaded with sound files from https://www.soundsofintent.app/count-me-in

Motif-Makers

- Wood block(s)
- Keyboard(s), glockenspiel(s), chime bars, tablet(s) with software that enables different pitches to be played
- A set of bird whistles

Music-Makers

- Keyboard(s), recorder(s), other wind instrument(s), tablet(s)
- Guitar(s), ukulele(s), bass guitar(s)
- Microphone(s) and amplifier(s)

Additional items

Winter Lament can be used as the basis for multisensory work. For example, you could start in a darkened room, and keep the lights low until the end of Verse 5, when the cheerier mood could be conveyed through brighter lighting as the dawn chorus gets underway. Air could be blown from a fan or wafted from a parachute to remind participants of the wind. You could put cold water in bowls so participants could immerse their hands or feet in them and feel the temperature. Think of using water sprays as a reminder of rain. Trays of dried leaves could be provided for participants to stir with their hands or scrunch underfoot or crush with the wheels of their wheelchairs. The sound of footsteps in the snow could be made by pummelling cornflour wrapped in a cloth.

Strategies

Try listening to *Winter Lament* a number of times over several days before encouraging participants to engage in an active way. This will help them to get to know the sounds, patterns, motifs, melodies and harmonies that are used. This approach is appropriate because in musical development – just as in aural traditions – listening precedes active participation. Individual parts can be practised one-to-one, and then in pairs or small groups, before attempting to bring the whole texture together.

With each verse, using the backing track, start with sound-makers, then pattern-makers and motif-makers before bringing music-makers in with the main melody. The arrangements are fully inclusive: everyone can join in, whatever their level of musical development. Some participants may engage with the music only sporadically, but whatever happens, the backing track will hold things together.

Links to other areas of experience and learning

In schools and colleges, *Winter Lament* can be linked to other areas of the curriculum, including geography (the seasons and the weather), chemistry (water as a liquid and in frozen forms) and ecology (the dawn chorus).

Winte[r]

Sound-Makers

During Verses 1–4

Enable participants to play bell-like instruments tuned to D or A, to make sustained sounds at any point in the Verses 1–4 of the song.

- chime bar
- hand bell
- tubular bells
- glock

Or help them make similar sounds by activating digitally recorded resonant sounds using gesture recognition technology such as that available on tablets and using beams,

- beam
- tablet

or by using switches or eye gaze technology.

- switch
- eye gaze

During Verse 5

Encourage participants to play the cymbal whenever they wish, if possible getting louder towards the end of the verse.

- cymbal

Introduction

↓

Verse 1
It's wintertime.
It rains and snows
Upon my face
A north wind blows.

Verse 2
It's wintertime.
The puddles freeze
With leaves that blew off
Bare-branched trees.

Verse 3
It's wintertime.
The freezing rain
And hail drum on
The windowpane.

Verse 4
It's wintertime.
Snow packs the ground,
Where footsteps make
A scrunching sound.

Verse 5
It's wintertime.
The world is grey.
But birds still sing
At break of day.

Copyright material from Ockelford, Gray, Cohen and Mai (2023), *Count Me In!*, Routledge

ament

Sound-Makers

- Sounds of the wind blowing and rain falling
- Sounds of ice cracking
- Repeated sounds of hail drumming on a windowpane
- Repeated sounds of footsteps on packed snow
- Medley of different bird songs

After Verse 1

Encourage participants to trigger digitally recorded sounds of wind or rain using touchscreens or beams.

tablet

beam

Participants may be able to vocalise rain-like sounds, which can be amplified and enhanced using effects such as reverberation, and repeated using a loop pedal.

mic

After Verse 2

Some participants may be able to trigger the sounds of ice cracking using switches or eye gaze technology.

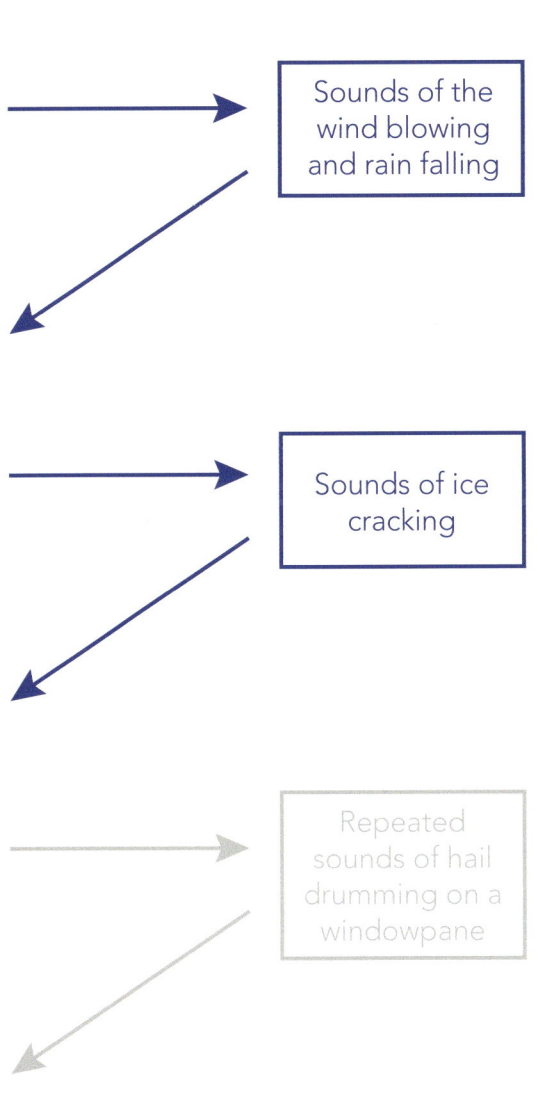

switch   eye gaze

Copyright material from Ockelford, Gray, Cohen and Mai (2023), *Count Me In!*, Routledge

Pattern-Makers

During each verse

Encourage participants to join in the slow, regular pulse of the song on a large (bass) drum, counting 1, 2, 3, 4.

1 2 3 4 **1** 2 3 4

boom — boom

bass drum

Show participants how to play a quicker beat on the cow bell that is twice the speed as that on the drum.

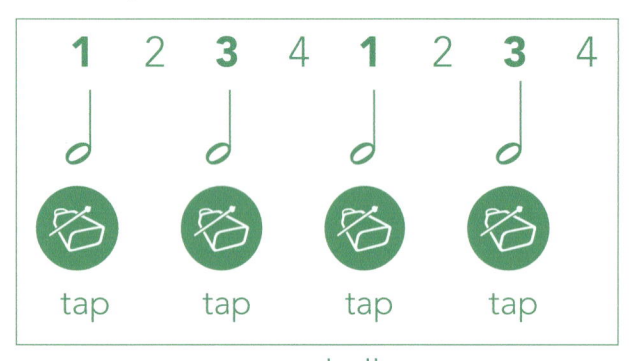

1 2 **3** 4 **1** 2 **3** 4

tap tap tap tap

cow bell

They may be able to play a quicker beat yet, with one strike of the wood block (for example) on each syllable of the vocal line.

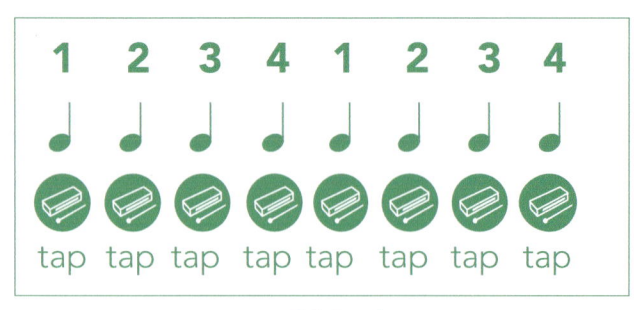

1 2 3 4 1 2 3 4

tap tap tap tap tap tap tap tap

wood block

Similar patterns can be made using switches.

Introduction
↓

Verse 1
It's wintertime.
It rains and snows
Upon my face
A north wind blows.

Verse 2
It's wintertime.
The puddles freeze
With leaves that blew off
Bare-branched trees.

Verse 3
It's wintertime.
The freezing rain
And hail drum on
The windowpane.

Verse 4
It's wintertime.
Snow packs the ground,
Where footsteps make
A scrunching sound.

Verse 5
It's wintertime.
The world is grey.
But birds still sing
At break of day.

Pattern-Makers

After Verse 3

Help participants to trigger single sounds of hail hitting a window or conservatory roof using tablets or switches, and repeat the sounds to make patterns. Or assist them in making similar patterns using claves.

- Sounds of the wind blowing and rain falling
- Sounds of ice cracking
- **Repeated sounds of hail drumming on a windowpane**

switch — sound of hailstones repeatedly hitting a window

claves — clack clack clack clack

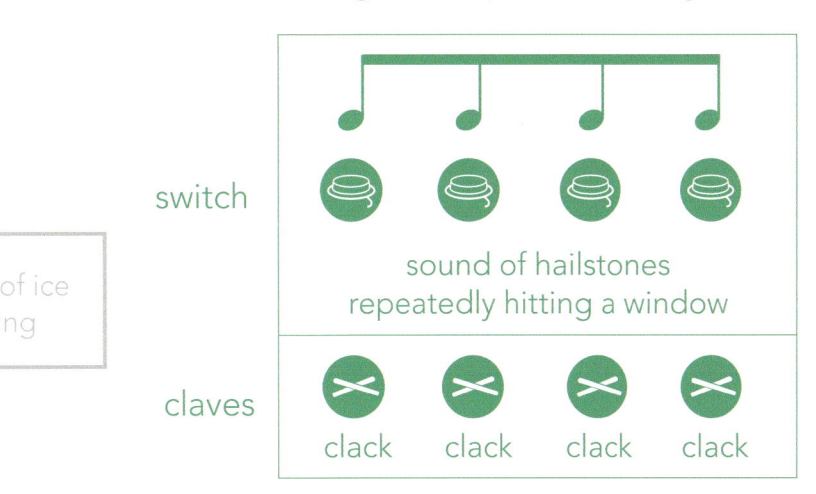

After Verse 4

Show participants how to trigger single sounds of footsteps in the snow using tablets or switches and how to repeat the sounds to make patterns. Some may be able to make similar patterns using a cabasa.

- **Repeated sounds of footsteps on packed snow**
- Medley of different bird songs

tablet — sound of footsteps in the snow

cabasa — scrunch scrunch

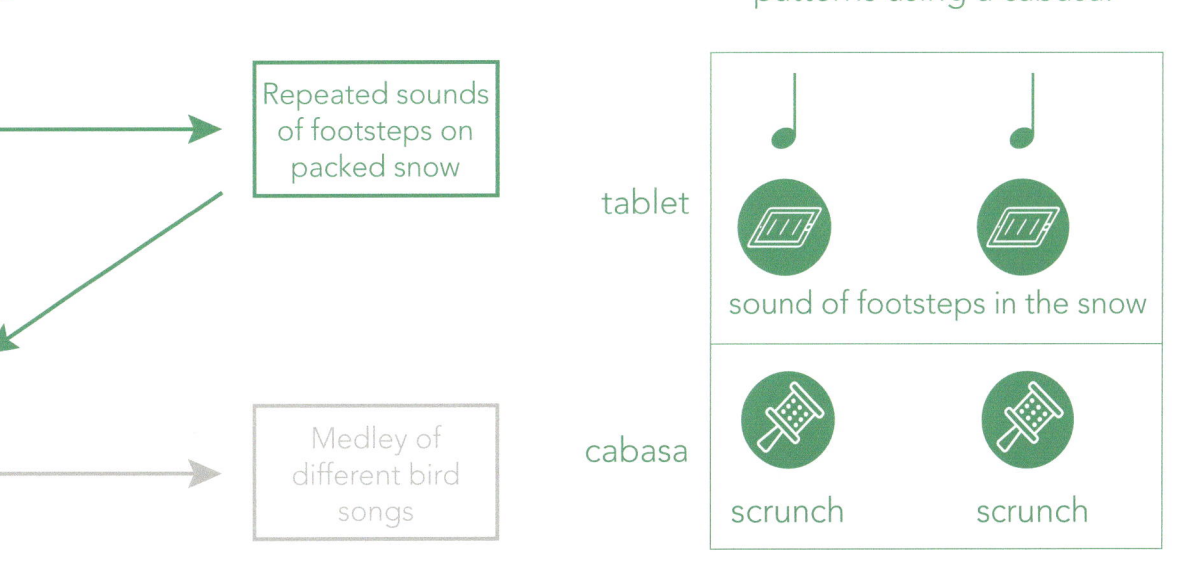

Copyright material from Ockelford, Gray, Cohen and Mai (2023), *Count Me In!*, Routledge

Winter

Motif-Makers

During each verse

Offer support to participants to join in with the steady beat of the song with short repeated rhythms on the wood block. To help keep the rhythm on track, try thinking of words that fit. For example:

'it's win – ter' [rest]

wood block

Verses 2–4

Show them how to play a slow ascending pattern of four notes on a melody instrument, such as a glockenspiel, keyboard or tablet, or by using four chime bars.

1	2	3	4	1	2	3	4
A				B♭			
1	2	3	4	1	2	3	4
C				D			

glock · tablet · chime bar · keys

Names of notes on a keyboard

Introduction
↓

Verse 1
It's wintertime.
It rains and snows
Upon my face
A north wind blows.

Verse 2
It's wintertime.
The puddles freeze
With leaves that blew off
Bare-branched trees.

Verse 3
It's wintertime.
The freezing rain
And hail drum on
The windowpane.

Verse 4
It's wintertime.
Snow packs the ground,
Where footsteps make
A scrunching sound.

Verse 5
It's wintertime.
The world is grey.
But birds still sing
At break of day.

Copyright material from Ockelford, Gray, Cohen and Mai (2023), *Count Me In!*, Routledge

Motif-Makers

After Verse 5

Demonstrate to participants how to connect various birdsongs together in different ways, choosing from digital collections of sounds triggered by buttons on computers or by using the touch screens of tablets or phones.

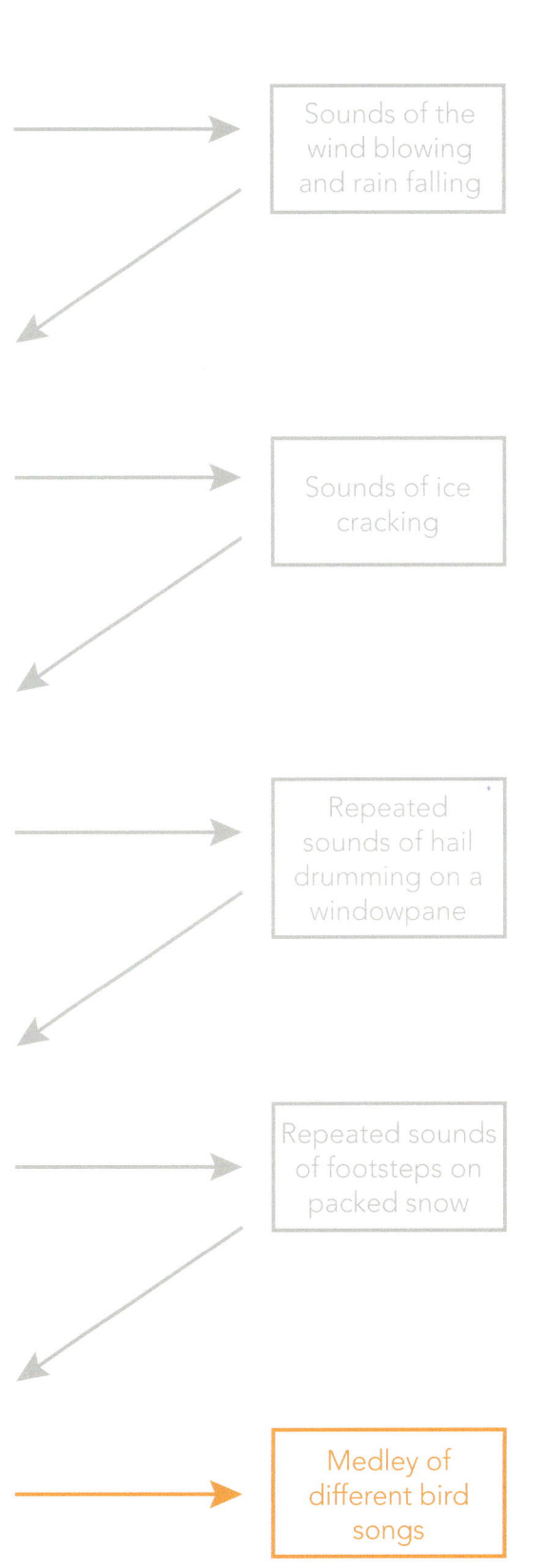

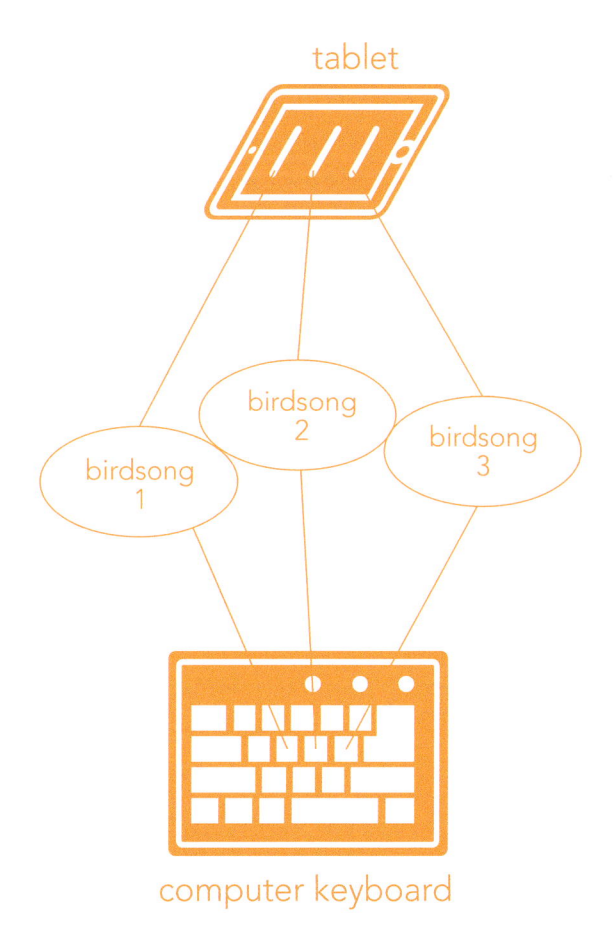

tablet

birdsong 1
birdsong 2
birdsong 3

computer keyboard

Or it may be possible for them to use different bird whistles, if they are available.

tweet   warble   whistle

Sounds of the wind blowing and rain falling

Sounds of ice cracking

Repeated sounds of hail drumming on a windowpane

Repeated sounds of footsteps on packed snow

Medley of different bird songs

Copyright material from Ockelford, Gray, Cohen and Mai (2023), *Count Me In!*, Routledge

Winter

```
Introduction
    ↓
Verse 1
It's wintertime.
It rains and snows
Upon my face
A north wind blows.          →  Sounds of the wind blowing and rain falling

Verse 2
It's wintertime.
The puddles freeze
With leaves that blew off
Bare-branched trees.         →  Sounds of ice cracking

Verse 3
It's wintertime.
The freezing rain
And hail drum on
The windowpane.              →  Repeated sounds of hail drumming on a windowpane

Verse 4
It's wintertime.
Snow packs the ground,
Where footsteps make
A scrunching sound.          →  Repeated sounds of footsteps on packed snow

Verse 5
It's wintertime.
The world is grey.
But birds still sing
At break of day.             →  Medley of different bird songs
```

Music-Makers

Encourage participants to sing or play the tune on a melody instrument (such as a keyboard or recorder). Play the bass line on a keyboard or bass guitar. Play the chords on a keyboard, guitar or ukulele.

keys — recorder — bass — guitar — ukulele

During Verses 1–4

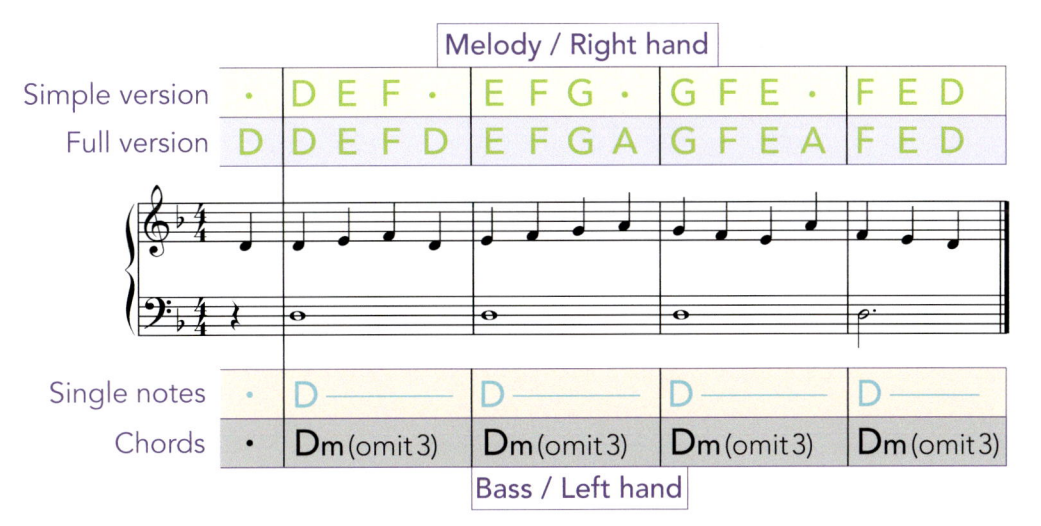

Melody / Right hand

Simple version	· D E F	· E F G	· G F E	· F E D
Full version	D D E F D	E F G A	G F E A	F E D

Single notes	· D ——	D ——	D ——	D ——
Chords	· Dm (omit 3)	Dm (omit 3)	Dm (omit 3)	Dm (omit 3)

Bass / Left hand

During Verse 5

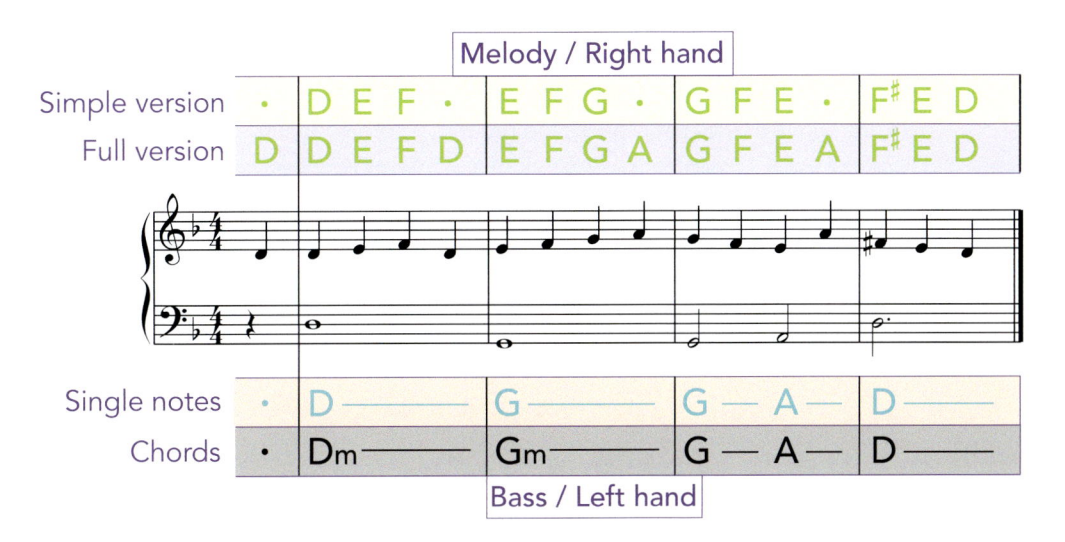

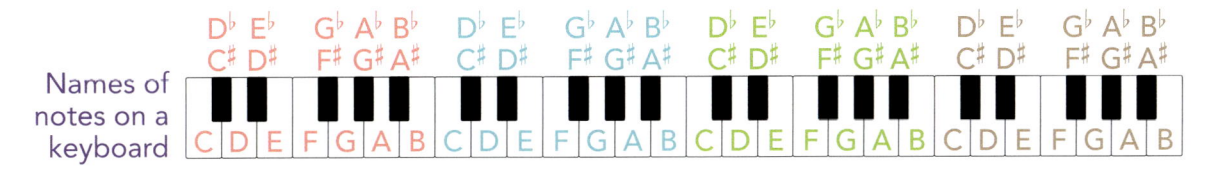

Melody / Right hand

Simple version	· D E F	· E F G	· G F E	· F♯ E D
Full version	D D E F D	E F G A	G F E A	F♯ E D

Single notes	· D ——	G ——	G — A	D ——
Chords	· Dm ——	Gm ——	G — A	D ——

Bass / Left hand

Names of notes on a keyboard:
C♯ D♯ F♯ G♯ A♯ — C♯ D♯ F♯ G♯ A♯ — C♯ D♯ F♯ G♯ A♯ — C♯ D♯ F♯ G♯ A♯ — C♯ D♯ F♯ G♯ A♯
D♭ E♭ G♭ A♭ B♭ — D♭ E♭ G♭ A♭ B♭ — D♭ E♭ G♭ A♭ B♭ — D♭ E♭ G♭ A♭ B♭ — D♭ E♭ G♭ A♭ B♭
C D E F G A B — C D E F G A B — C D E F G A B — C D E F G A B — C D E F G A B

Copyright material from Ockelford, Gray, Cohen and Mai (2023), *Count Me In!*, Routledge

Winter

Score for music teachers to use

1. It's winter time. It rains and snows up-on my face a cold wind blows.

2. It's winter time. The puddles freeze with leaves that blew off bare-branched trees.

3. It's winter time. The freezing rain and hail drum on the window-pane.

4. It's winter time. Snow packs the ground, where foot-steps make a scrunching sound.

5. It's winter time. The world is grey, but birds still sing at break of day.

Lament

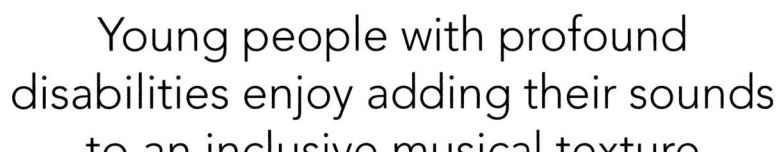

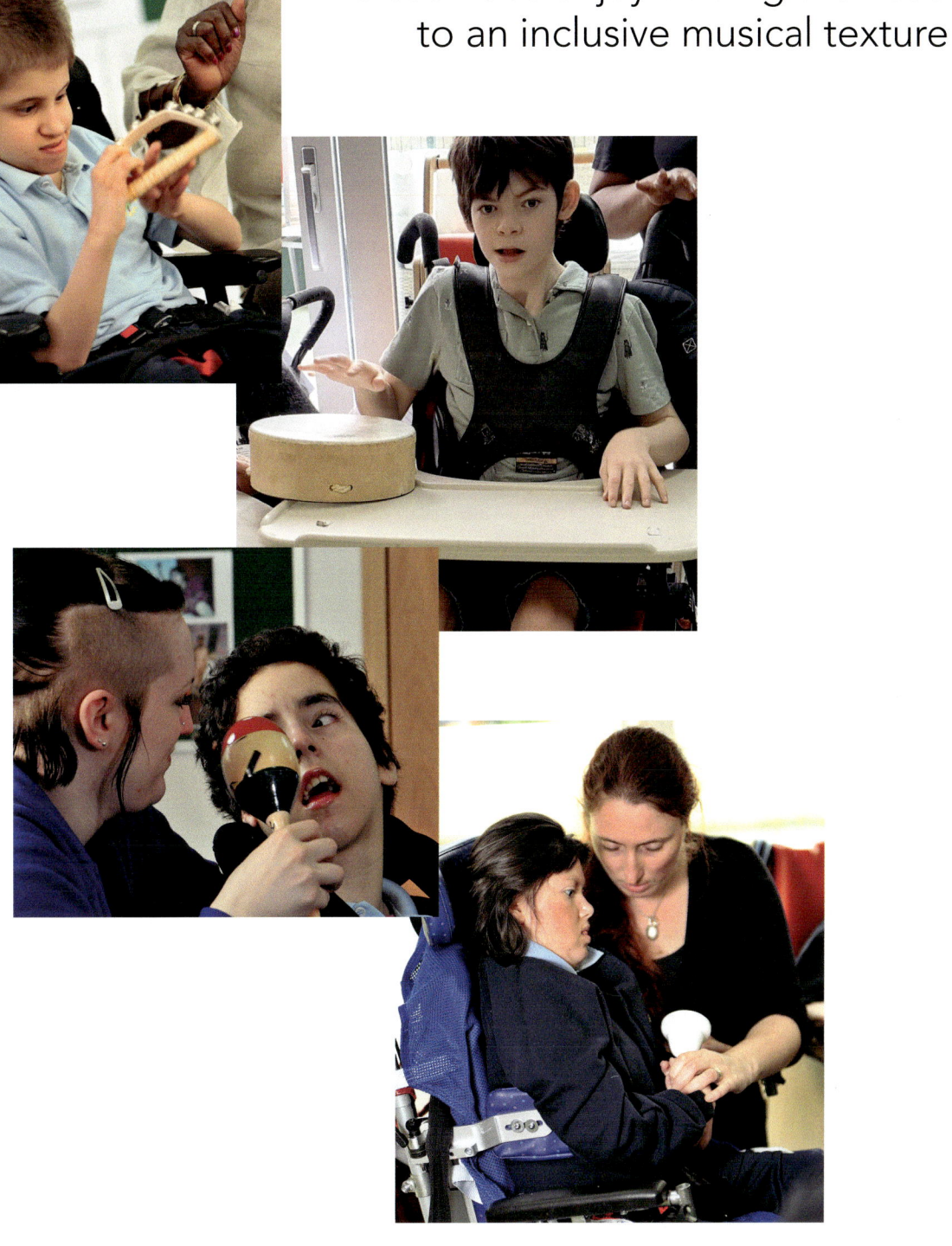

Young people with profound disabilities enjoy adding their sounds to an inclusive musical texture

Spring

Introduction

Spring Serenade borrows the opening two themes of Antonio Vivaldi's concerto *La Primavera*, which means 'spring' in English. Vivaldi was an Italian composer of the Baroque period, and *La Primavera* is the first in a set of concertos known as *The Four Seasons*. The concertos were written around 1720, when Vivaldi was working in Mantua. They were meant to be played by a small string orchestra with solo violin and a harpsichord. Each movement was published with an accompanying poem that guides listeners to imagine a particular scene. Music like this, which deliberately sets out to paint a picture in sound, is known as 'programme music', and, together, *The Four Seasons* make up the first well-known example in Western classical music. The opening of the poem associated with *La Primavera*, in English, is as follows:

Springtime is upon us.
The birds celebrate its return with festive song.

Spring Serenade picks up on the idea of joyous spring birdsong and sets new words to the opening violin melody in each of four verses. The first mentions a robin; the second, a sparrow; the third, a song thrush; and the fourth brings to mind all the birds that sing in the spring. Each verse has parts for sound-makers, pattern-makers, motif-makers and music-makers. So all participants, no matter what their level of musical development, can join in together. Between verses there are sections where players can use digital recordings of birds singing to create their own imaginary rural soundscapes. The first is particularly suited to sound-makers, the second will work well for pattern-makers, the third is designed especially for motif-makers, and the fourth is for music-makers. However, *Spring Serenade* can be used flexibly, and the sounds of birdsong will fit wherever participants choose!

Musical resources required

Choose from the following, according to participants' abilities, preferences and needs:

Sound-Makers

- Triangle(s), tambourine(s)
- Control of digitally recorded triangle and tambourine sounds, and robins singing through
    - gesture recognition technology (tablets/beams)
    - eye gaze technology
    - switch(es)

   that are loaded with sound files from https://www.soundsofintent.app/count-me-in

Pattern-Makers

- Drum(s), chime bar(s) tuned to E, keyboard(s), glockenspiel(s), recorder(s), tablet(s) with the note E
- Pattern-making through individually recorded sparrow chirps using a switch or switches that are loaded with sound files from https://www.soundsofintent.app/count-me-in

Motif-Makers

- Wood block(s), tambourine(s)
- Control of digitally recorded song thrush motifs, that are loaded with sound files from https://www.soundsofintent.app/count-me-in activated through a computer keyboard or tablet

Music-Makers

- Keyboard(s), recorder(s), other wind instrument(s), tablet(s)
- Guitar(s), ukulele(s), bass guitar(s)
- Microphone(s) and amplifier(s)

Additional items

Spring Serenade lends itself well to multisensory activities. For example, the scents of spring such as newly mown grass and cherry blossom could be introduced. Spring flowers could be shown to participants, and pictures of spring scenes shown on a large screen. Some may enjoy dancing to the music – perhaps around a maypole. On a warm spring day, the song could be performed outdoors.

Strategies

If possible, listen to *Spring Serenade* on several occasions before encouraging participants to join in. This will help them become familiar with the sounds, patterns, motifs, melodies and harmonies that are used. Always remember that listening precedes active participation. Individual participants' contributions can be practised one-to-one, and then in pairs or small groups, before you attempt to bring the whole texture together.

Use the backing track at the beginning of each verse to introduce sound-makers with their parts, then pattern-makers and shape-makers, before encouraging music-makers to come in with the main tune. Whatever their capacity to engage with music, everyone can join in. If some participants are not present or choose not to play or sing, the backing track will hold things together.

Spring Serenade can be used to introduce participants to Vivaldi's original concerto, *La Primavera*, and the remaining pieces in *The Four Seasons*.

Links to other areas of experience and learning

In schools and colleges, *Spring Serenade* has potential links to other curricular areas, particularly physical geography (the seasons), human geography (festivals associated with spring) and biology (growth and renewal as part of the life cycle).

Spring

Sound-Makers

During each verse

Encourage participants to ding the triangle from time to time. Show them how to make a jingling sound by wiggling the beater to and fro in one of its corners.

triangle

Help them to strike the tambourine every now and then, or shake it to make a silvery jangling sound.

tambourine

Or assist them to make similar sounds by activating digitally recorded tambourine or triangle sounds using gesture recognition technology such as that available on tablets or by using beams,

beam   **tablet**

or by using switches or eye gaze technology.

switch   **eye gaze**

Verse 1

Now spring time is here,
The birds sing loud and clear.
Can you hear the robin singing?

The robin is singing,
His song good cheer is bringing,
Is bringing,
Now let us play along.

Verse 2

Now spring time is here,
The birds sing loud and clear.
Can you hear the sparrow singing?

The sparrow is singing,
His song good cheer is bringing,
Is bringing,
Now let us play along.

Verse 3

Now spring time is here,
The birds sing loud and clear.
Can you hear the song thrush singing?

The song thrush is singing,
His song good cheer is bringing,
Is bringing,
Now let us play along.

Verse 4

Now spring time is here,
The birds sing loud and clear.
Can you hear the birds singing?

The birds are singing,
Their song good cheer is bringing,
Is bringing,
Now let us play along.

Copyright material from Ockelford, Gray, Cohen and Mai (2023), *Count Me In!*, Routledge

Serenade

Sound-Makers
After Verse 1

Enable participants to trigger pre-recorded sounds of robins singing

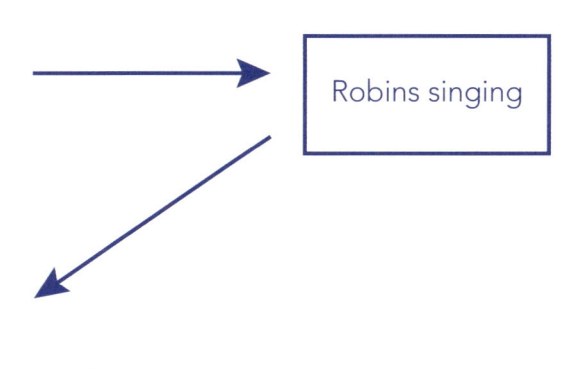

Robins singing

Sparrows singing

Song thrushes singing

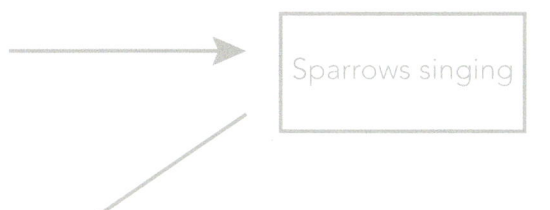

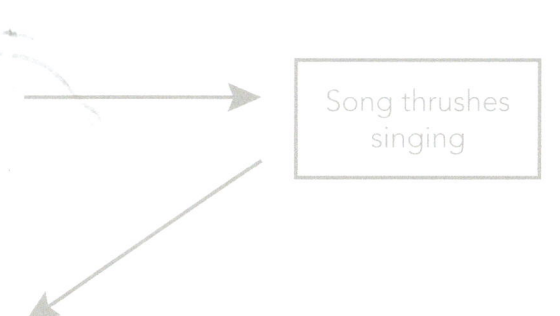

Birds singing

using a switch

or eye gaze technology,

or by using a beam

or a tablet.

Spring

Pattern-Makers

During each verse

Support participants in joining in the regular beats ofn the song on the drum.

1	2	3	4
bang	bang	bang	bang

drum

Or help them to play long notes on a chime, keyboard, glockenspiel, recorder, guitar or tablet.

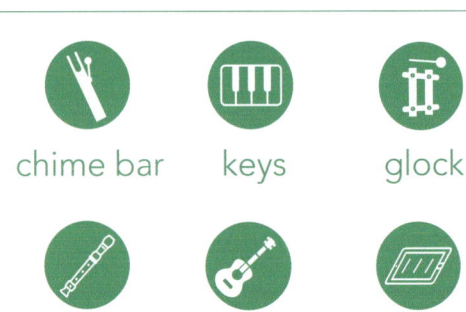

1 2 3 4 **1** 2 3 4
E ——————— E ———————

chime bar   keys   glock

recorder   guitar   tablet

Verse 1
Now spring time is here,
The birds sing loud and clear.
Can you hear the robin singing?

The robin is singing,
His song good cheer is bringing,
Is bringing,
Now let us play along.

Verse 2
Now spring time is here,
The birds sing loud and clear.
Can you hear the sparrow singing?

The sparrow is singing,
His song good cheer is bringing,
Is bringing,
Now let us play along.

Verse 3
Now spring time is here,
The birds sing loud and clear.
Can you hear the song thrush singing?

The song thrush is singing,
His song good cheer is bringing,
Is bringing,
Now let us play along.

Verse 4
Now spring time is here,
The birds sing loud and clear.
Can you hear the birds singing?

The birds are singing,
Their song good cheer is bringing,
Is bringing,
Now let us play along.

Copyright material from Ockelford, Gray, Cohen and Mai (2023), *Count Me In!*, Routledge

Serenade

Pattern-Makers

After Verse 2

Show participants how to trigger single sparrow chirps

using tablets or switches and how to repeat the sounds to make patterns.

Robins singing

Sparrows singing

The chirps could be quite rapid

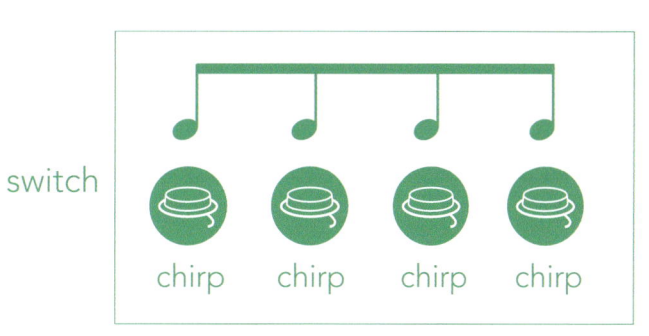

switch | chirp chirp chirp chirp

rapid single sparrow chirps

Song thrushes singing

or somewhat slower.

tablet | chirp chirp chirp

slower sparrow chirps

Birds singing

Spring

Motif-Makers

During each verse

Show participants how to play a repeated rhythm on the wood block. Saying short groups of words may help keep the rhythm on track. For example:

'birds   sing – ing'

wood block

Encourage them to try other rhythms on other instruments. For example:

'spring   is   here'

tambourine

Show them how to play the rhythms in time with the music.

Verse 1
Now spring time is here,
The birds sing loud and clear.
Can you hear the robin singing?

The robin is singing,
His song good cheer is bringing,
Is bringing,
Now let us play along.

Verse 2
Now spring time is here,
The birds sing loud and clear.
Can you hear the sparrow singing?

The sparrow is singing,
His song good cheer is bringing,
Is bringing,
Now let us play along.

Verse 3
Now spring time is here,
The birds sing loud and clear.
Can you hear the song thrush singing?

The song thrush is singing,
His song good cheer is bringing,
Is bringing,
Now let us play along.

Verse 4
Now spring time is here,
The birds sing loud and clear.
Can you hear the birds singing?

The birds are singing,
Their song good cheer is bringing,
Is bringing,
Now let us play along.

Serenade

Motif-Makers

After Verse 3

When song thrushes sing, they always repeat each short phrase two or three times.

Encourage participants to do the same with song thrush motifs that have been downloaded onto tablets or computers.

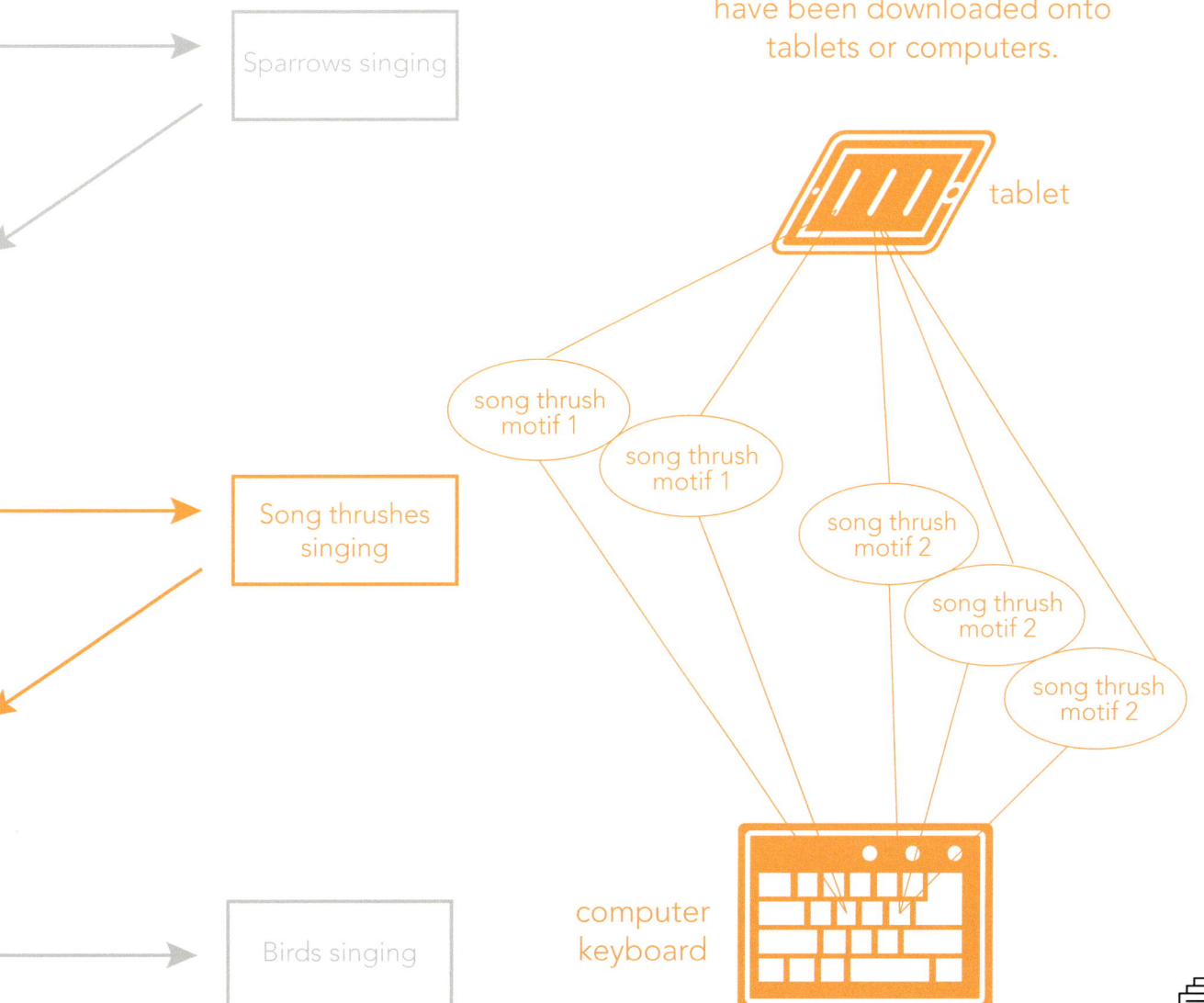

- Robins singing
- Sparrows singing
- **Song thrushes singing**
  - song thrush motif 1
  - song thrush motif 1
  - song thrush motif 2
  - song thrush motif 2
  - song thrush motif 2
  - tablet
  - computer keyboard
- Birds singing

Spring

Verse 1

Now spring time is here,
The birds sing loud and clear.
Can you hear the robin singing?

The robin is singing,
His song good cheer is bringing,
Is bringing,
Now let us play along.

→ Robins singing

Verse 2

Now spring time is here,
The birds sing loud and clear.
Can you hear the sparrow singing?

The sparrow is singing,
His song good cheer is bringing,
Is bringing,
Now let us play along.

→ Sparrows singing

Verse 3

Now spring time is here,
The birds sing loud and clear.
Can you hear the song thrush singing?

The song thrush is singing,
His song good cheer is bringing,
Is bringing,
Now let us play along.

→ Song thrushes singing

Verse 4

Now spring time is here,
The birds sing loud and clear.
Can you hear the birds singing?

The birds are singing,
Their song good cheer is bringing,
Is bringing,
Now let us play along.

→ Birds singing

Music-Makers

After Verse 4

Before a performance of *Spring Serenade*, help participants create a short soundscape of digitally recorded bird song using an app such as GarageBand. Replay the montage of sounds after Verse 4.

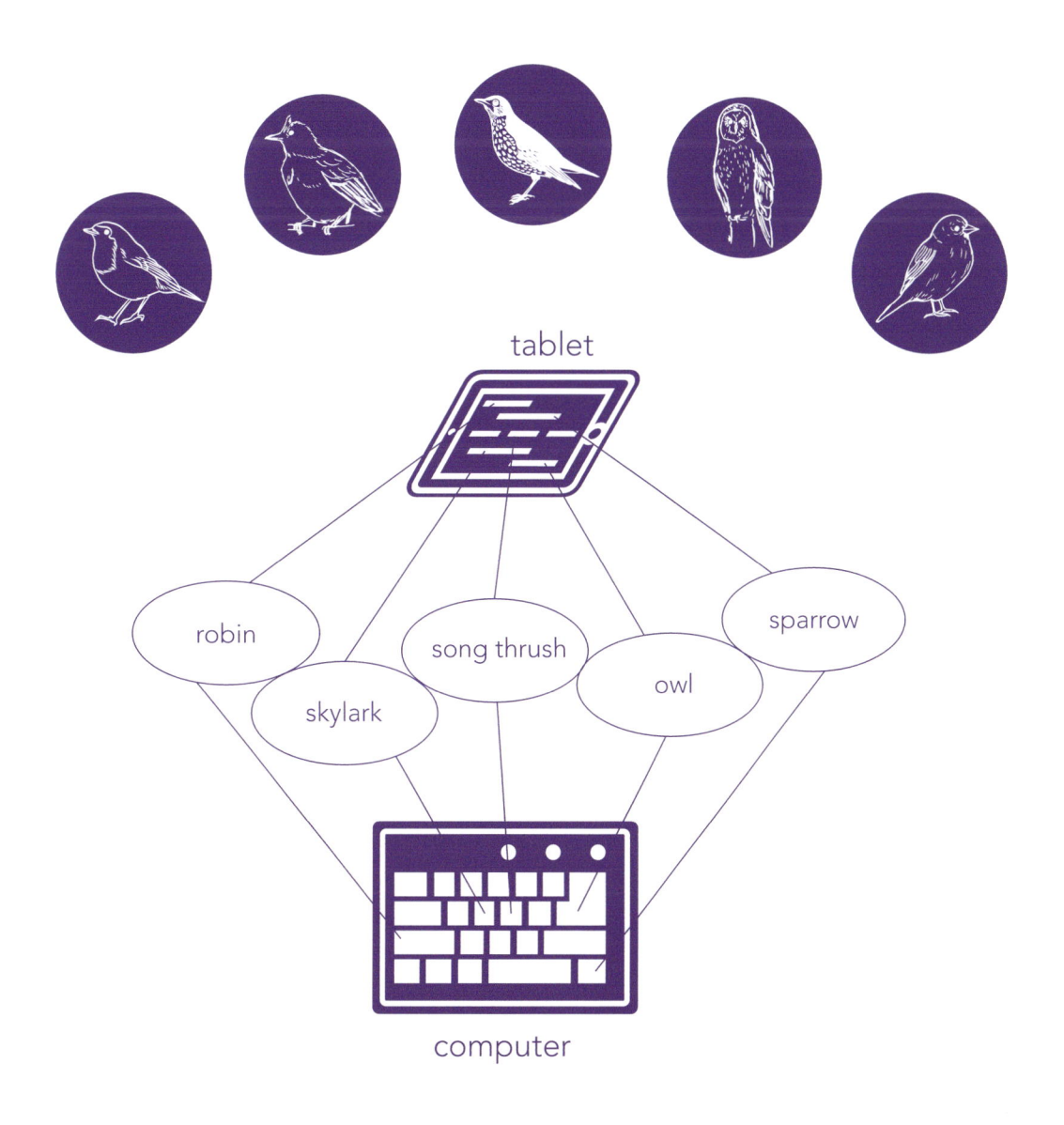

tablet

robin • skylark • song thrush • owl • sparrow

computer

Spring

Music-Makers

During each verse

Encourage participants to sing or play the tune on a melody instrument (such as a keyboard or recorder). Play the bass line on a keyboard or bass guitar. They could play the chords on a keyboard, guitar or ukulele, using simpler versions (in bold) if preferred.

keys · recorder · bass · guitar · ukulele

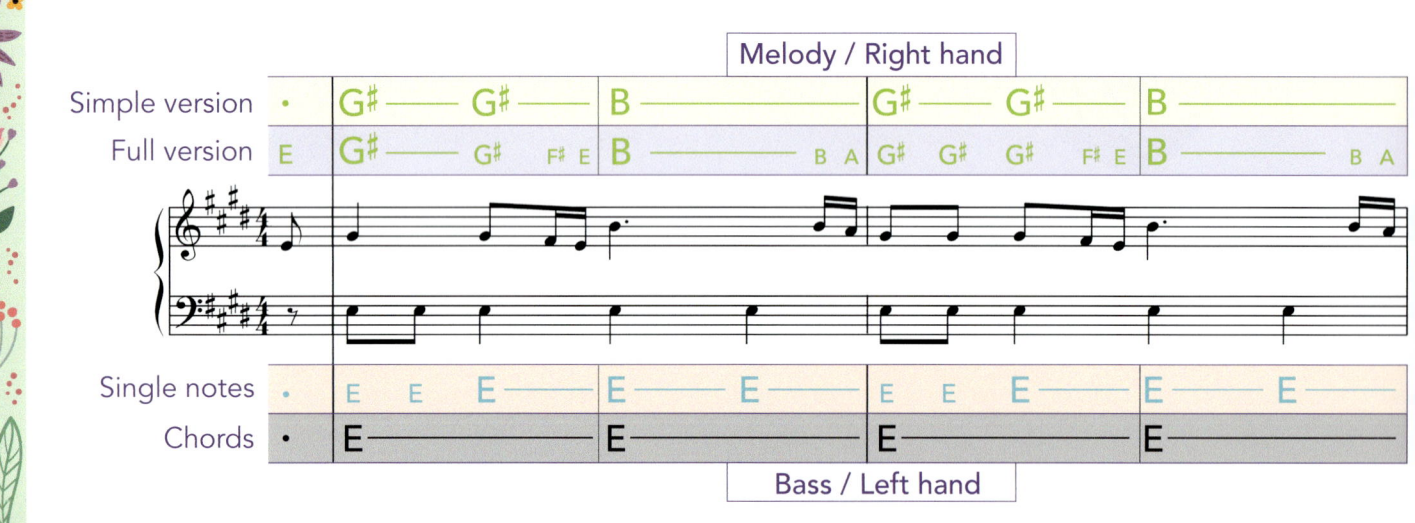

Melody / Right hand

Simple version	·	G# — G#	B	G# — G#	B	
Full version	E	G# — G# F# E	B — B A	G# G# G# F# E	B — B A	

Single notes	· E E	E	E E	E E	E E
Chords	· E———	E———	E———	E———	

Bass / Left hand

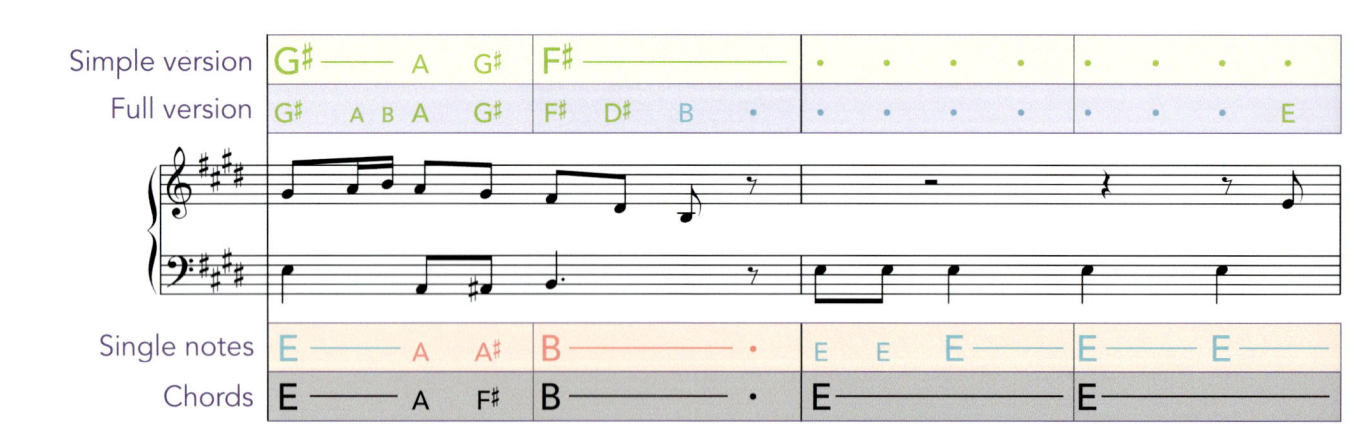

Simple version	G# — A G#	F#	·	·	·	·	·	·
Full version	G# A B A G#	F# D# B	·	·	·	·	·	E

Single notes	E A A#	B ·	E E	E	E E	
Chords	E——— A F#	B ·	E———		E———	

49

Copyright material from Ockelford, Gray, Cohen and Mai (2023), *Count Me In!*, Routledge

Serenade

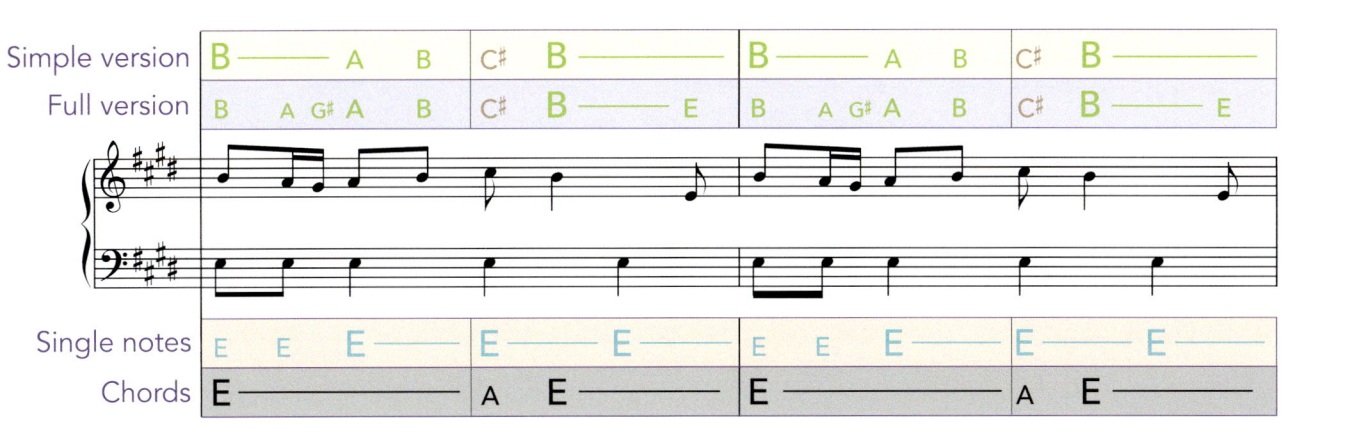

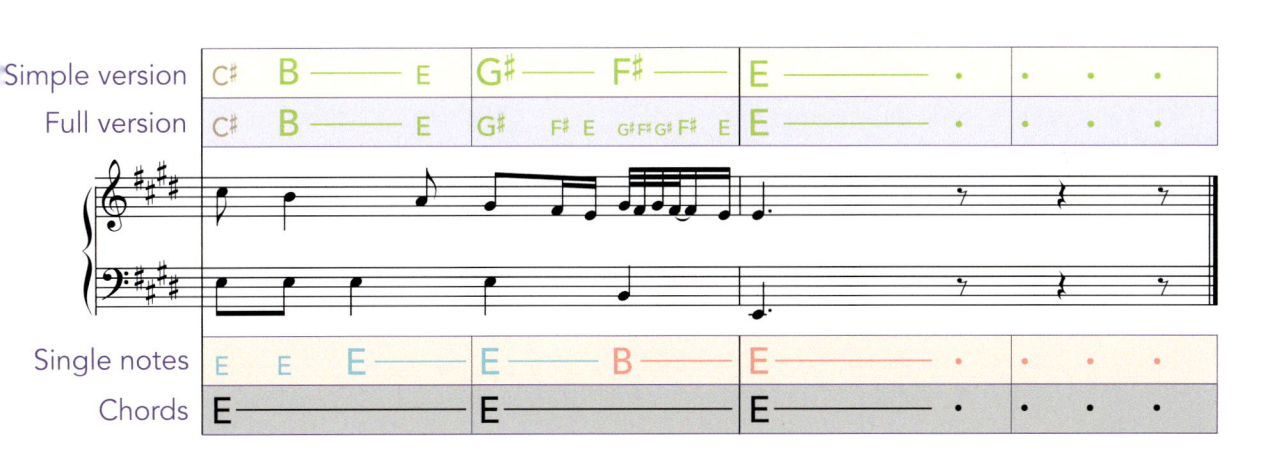

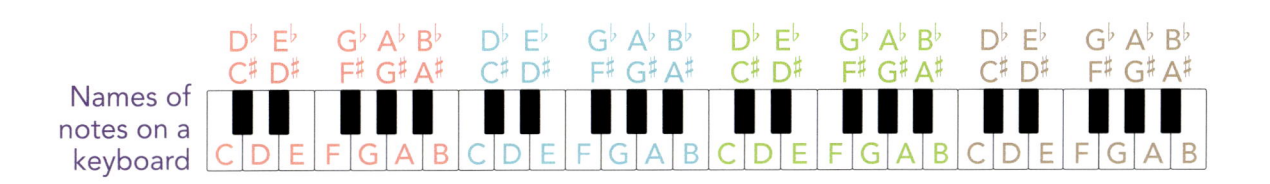

Spring

Score for music teachers to use

Voice and keyboard

Lyrics:

Now spring-time is here, the birds sing loud and clear. Can you

1. hear the robin singing? The robin is singing, His
2. hear the sparrow singing? The sparrow is singing, His
3. hear the song thrush singing? The song thrush is singing, His
4. hear the birds singing? The birds are singing, Their

song good cheer is bring-ing, is bring-ing, now let us play a-long.

Serenade

Keyboard only

Summer

Introduction

Summer Jig is based on the medieval English round '*Sumer is Icumen in*', which means 'Summer is arriving'. It is around 900 years old, dating from the mid-thirteenth century. A 'round' is a song that can be sung by two or more people, starting at different times. So, in effect, the tune forms its own accompaniment. Some well-known children's songs are rounds, including *Frère Jacques* and *London's Burning*. *Sumer is Icumen in* is actually made up of two rounds that happen at the same time – one for higher voices and one for lower voices. The round for lower voices is short, and is repeated several times, while the round with the higher voices, which carry the main tune, is much longer. The original words, written in 'Middle English' have been modernised in *Summer Jig*, though the metre and rhyming structure are maintained, so the fit with the music is the same.

Summer Jig has one verse, which is repeated. There are separate sets of resources for sound-makers, pattern-makers, motif-makers and music-makers. This means that everyone can join in together. Before the first verse, after the second, and between the two, there are three improvised sections, where players and singers can contribute in a wide range of different ways to the rural soundscapes that are downloadable on the website.

Musical resources required

Choose from the following, according to participants' abilities, preferences and needs:

Sound-Makers

- Chime bar(s), hand bell(s), tubular bells, glockenspiel(s)
- Control of similar digitally recorded sounds, and rural sounds such as a stream, rustling leaves, and animal and bird sounds, through
    - gesture recognition technology (tablets/beams)
    - eye gaze technology
    - switch(es)

  that are loaded with sound files from https://www.soundsofintent.app/count-me-in or elsewhere
- Microphone(s), amplifier(s) with effect unit(s)

Pattern-Makers

- Frame drum(s), tambourine(s)
- Pattern-making through individual drum or tambourine sounds using a switch or a tablet loaded with sound files from https://www.soundsofintent.app/count-me-in

Motif-Makers

- Cowbell(s)
- Keyboard(s)

- Beam(s) and tablet(s) able to play C, D, F and G, and digitally recorded individual bird sounds, downloaded from https://www.soundsofintent.app/count-me-in or elsewhere
- Microphone(s), amplifier(s) with effect unit(s)

Music-Makers

- Keyboard(s), recorder(s) and/or other wind instrument(s), tablet(s)
- Guitar(s), ukulele(s), bass guitar(s)
- Computer or tablet with sequencing software such as GarageBand, preloaded with rural sounds such as a stream, rustling leaves, and animal and bird sounds, from https://www.soundsofintent.app/count-me-in or elsewhere
- Microphone(s) and amplifier(s)

Additional items

Summer Jig can be performed in a multisensory way, supplemented with pictures, videos and items from nature such as flowers and twigs from trees in blossom, which particpants can see, feel and smell. It may even be performed outside.

Strategies

It is best to listen to *Summer Jig* for a week or two before encouraging participants to join in. This will enable them to become familiar with the sounds, patterns, motifs, melodies and harmonies that are used. Always remember that listening is just as much a part of the musical experience as making sounds yourself.

Individual parts can be rehearsed one-to-one, and then in pairs or small groups, before you attempt to bring the whole texture together.

With each verse, the backing track will cue in sound-makers first, then pattern-makers and motif-makers (with the shorter round for lower voices) before music-makers come in with the main tune, which can also be sung or played as a round. The arrangements have parts for everyone, whatever their capacity to engage with music. If some members of the group are not present or elect not to play or sing, the backing track will hold things together.

Links to other areas of experience and learning

In schools and colleges, *Summer Jig* has potential links to other curricular areas, such as geography (the seasons) and history (life in medieval times in England).

Sound-Makers

During each verse

Enable participants to play bell-like instruments, tuned to C or G, to make sustained sounds at any point in the song, to fit with the drone on the backing track.

- chime bar
- hand bell
- tubular bells
- glock

Or help them make similar sounds by activating digitally recorded resonant sounds using gesture recognition technology such as that available on tablets and using beams,

- beam
- tablet

or by using switches or eye gaze technology.

- switch
- eye gaze

Lyrics (higher voices)

Summer is a-coming in,
Loudly sing cuckoo!
Seeds they grow and blossoms show
In woods that bud anew.
Sing Cuckoo!

Ewes bleat for their lambs
And cows look for their calves and moo.
Bullocks jump and deer thump,
So merry sing cuckoo!

Sing cuckoo now,
Merry sing cuckoo now
And sing it all anew.

Lyrics (lower voices)

Sing cuckoo now, sing cuckoo!
Sing cuckoo now, sing cuckoo!

Lyrics (higher voices)

Summer is a-coming in,
Loudly sing cuckoo!
Seeds they grow and blossoms show
In woods that bud anew.
Sing Cuckoo!

Ewes bleat for their lambs
And cows look for their calves and moo.
Bullocks jump and deer thump,
So merry sing cuckoo!

Sing cuckoo now,
Merry sing cuckoo now
And sing it all anew.

Lyrics (lower voices)

Sing cuckoo now, sing cuckoo!
Sing cuckoo now, sing cuckoo!

Copyright material from Ockelford, Gray, Cohen and Mai (2023), *Count Me In!*, Routledge

ig

Prelude
Rural Soundscape

Interlude
Rural Soundscape

Postlude
Rural Soundscape

Sound-Makers

In the Rural Soundscapes

Encourage participants to trigger pre-recorded sounds of the countryside, downloaded from the *Count Me In!* web pages or elsewhere, or recorded during a trip out. Sounds could include a tinkling stream, a gentle breeze, rustling leaves, and animal or bird sounds. These could be activated using a switch or eye gaze technology,

switch   eye gaze

or gesture recognition devices such as a tablet or beam.

tablet   beam

Some participants may contribute vocal sounds of their own to the soundscapes, that could be enhanced using a microphone, amplifier and effects unit.

mic

Copyright material from Ockelford, Gray, Cohen and Mai (2023), *Count Me In!*, Routledge

Summer

Pattern-Makers

During each verse

Show participants how to join in with the slower, regular beat of the song on a drum or other non-pitched percussion instrument. For example:

bang   bang

frame drum

Or help them to play with the quicker, jig-like beat, which has a longer note followed by a shorter one. For example:

play – ing,   play – ing

tambourine

Or encourage them to do the same with downloaded percussive sounds triggered by using a switch or a tablet.

switch   tablet

Lyrics (higher voices)

Summer is a-coming in,
Loudly sing cuckoo!
Seeds they grow and blossoms show
In woods that bud anew.
Sing Cuckoo!

Ewes bleat for their lambs
And cows look for their calves and moo.
Bullocks jump and deer thump,
So merry sing cuckoo!

Sing cuckoo now,
Merry sing cuckoo now
And sing it all anew.

Lyrics (lower voices)

Sing cuckoo now, sing cuckoo!
Sing cuckoo now, sing cuckoo!

Lyrics (higher voices)

Summer is a-coming in,
Loudly sing cuckoo!
Seeds they grow and blossoms show
In woods that bud anew.
Sing Cuckoo!

Ewes bleat for their lambs
And cows look for their calves and moo.
Bullocks jump and deer thump,
So merry sing cuckoo!

Sing cuckoo now,
Merry sing cuckoo now
And sing it all anew.

Lyrics (lower voices)

Sing cuckoo now, sing cuckoo!
Sing cuckoo now, sing cuckoo!

ig

Prelude
Rural Soundscape

Pattern-Makers

In the Rural Soundscapes

Enable participants to make regular patterns of birds singing, by repeatedly pressing a switch, touchscreen or computer key, loaded with a single digital tweet, at different speeds.

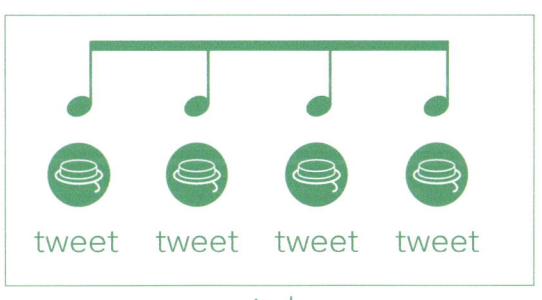

tweet tweet tweet tweet
switch

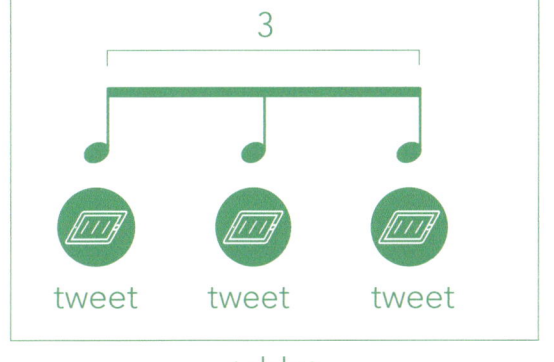

3
tweet tweet tweet
tablet

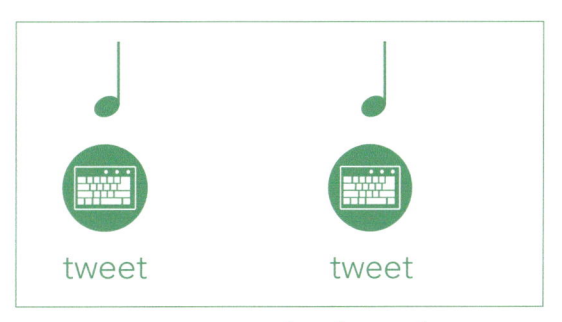

Interlude
Rural Soundscape

tweet tweet
computer keyboard

Postlude
Rural Soundscape

Copyright material from Ockelford, Gray, Cohen and Mai (2023), *Count Me In!*, Routledge

58

Summer

Motif-Makers

During each verse

Show participants how to join in with the lower voice parts singing or playing 'Sing cuckoo'. Try call and response activities. For example:

| 'Sing | cuck – oo' | [rest] |

cowbell

CALL

| C | D | C | [rest] |
| 'Sing | cuck – oo' | |

RESPONSE

| G | F | G | [rest] |
| 'Sing | cuck – oo' | |

mic · keys · beam · tablet

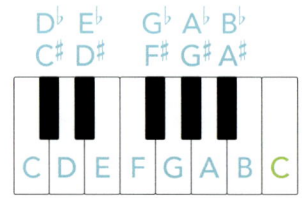

Names of notes on a keyboard (C D E F G A B C, with D♭/C♯, E♭/D♯, G♭/F♯, A♭/G♯, B♭/A♯)

Lyrics (higher voices)

Summer is a-coming in,
Loudly sing cuckoo!
Seeds they grow and blossoms show
In woods that bud anew.
Sing Cuckoo!

Ewes bleat for their lambs
And cows look for their calves and moo.
Bullocks jump and deer thump,
So merry sing cuckoo!

Sing cuckoo now,
Merry sing cuckoo now
And sing it all anew.

Lyrics (lower voices)

Sing cuckoo now, sing cuckoo!
Sing cuckoo now, sing cuckoo!

Lyrics (higher voices)

Summer is a-coming in,
Loudly sing cuckoo!
Seeds they grow and blossoms show
In woods that bud anew.
Sing Cuckoo!

Ewes bleat for their lambs
And cows look for their calves and moo.
Bullocks jump and deer thump,
So merry sing cuckoo!

Sing cuckoo now,
Merry sing cuckoo now
And sing it all anew.

Lyrics (lower voices)

Sing cuckoo now, sing cuckoo!
Sing cuckoo now, sing cuckoo!

ig

Prelude
Rural Soundscape

Motif-Makers

In the Rural Soundscapes

Demonstrate to participants how to connect different groups of digitally recorded rural sounds such as bird tweets and animal noises, choosing from collections of sounds triggered by keys on computers or the screens of tablets or phones.

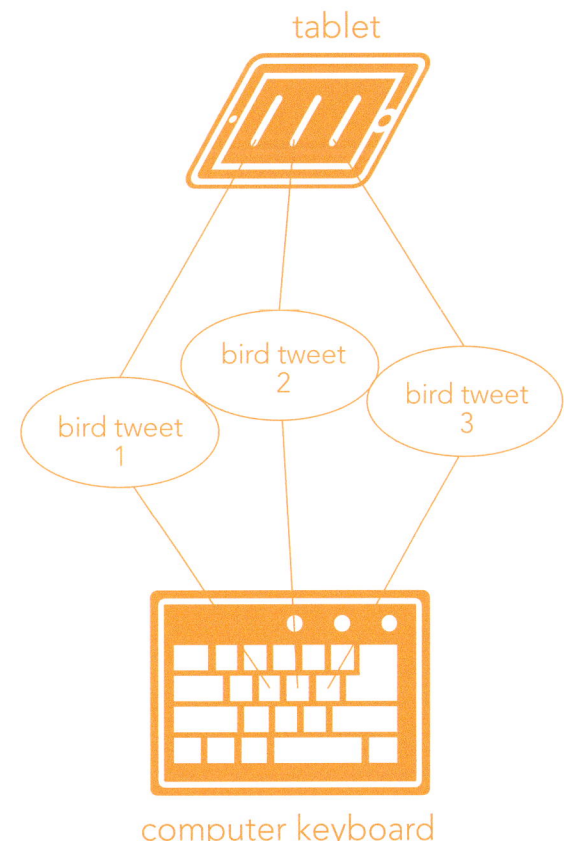

tablet

bird tweet 1 bird tweet 2 bird tweet 3

computer keyboard

Some participants may make and combine bird songs vocally, using a microphone and effects unit, if there is one available.

mic

Interlude
Rural Soundscape

Postlude
Rural Soundscape

Copyright material from Ockelford, Gray, Cohen and Mai (2023), *Count Me In!*, Routledge

Summer

Prelude
Rural Soundscape

Lyrics (higher voices)

Summer is a-coming in,
Loudly sing cuckoo!
Seeds they grow and blossoms show
In woods that bud anew.
Sing Cuckoo!

Ewes bleat for their lambs
And cows look for their calves and moo.
Bullocks jump and deer thump,
So merry sing cuckoo!

Sing cuckoo now,
Merry sing cuckoo now
And sing it all anew.

Lyrics (lower voices)

Sing cuckoo now, sing cuckoo!
Sing cuckoo now, sing cuckoo!

Interlude
Rural Soundscape

Lyrics (higher voices)

Summer is a-coming in,
Loudly sing cuckoo!
Seeds they grow and blossoms show
In woods that bud anew.
Sing Cuckoo!

Ewes bleat for their lambs
And cows look for their calves and moo.
Bullocks jump and deer thump,
So merry sing cuckoo!

Sing cuckoo now,
Merry sing cuckoo now
And sing it all anew.

Lyrics (lower voices)

Sing cuckoo now, sing cuckoo!
Sing cuckoo now, sing cuckoo!

Postlude
Rural Soundscape

Copyright material from Ockelford, Gray, Cohen and Mai (2023), *Count Me In!*, Routledge

Music-Makers

In the Rural Soundscapes

Before a performance of *Summer Jig*, assist participants in creating a short soundscape of digitally recorded rural sounds using an app such as GarageBand. Replay the montage of sounds during the improvised Prelude, Interlude and Postlude sections. For example:

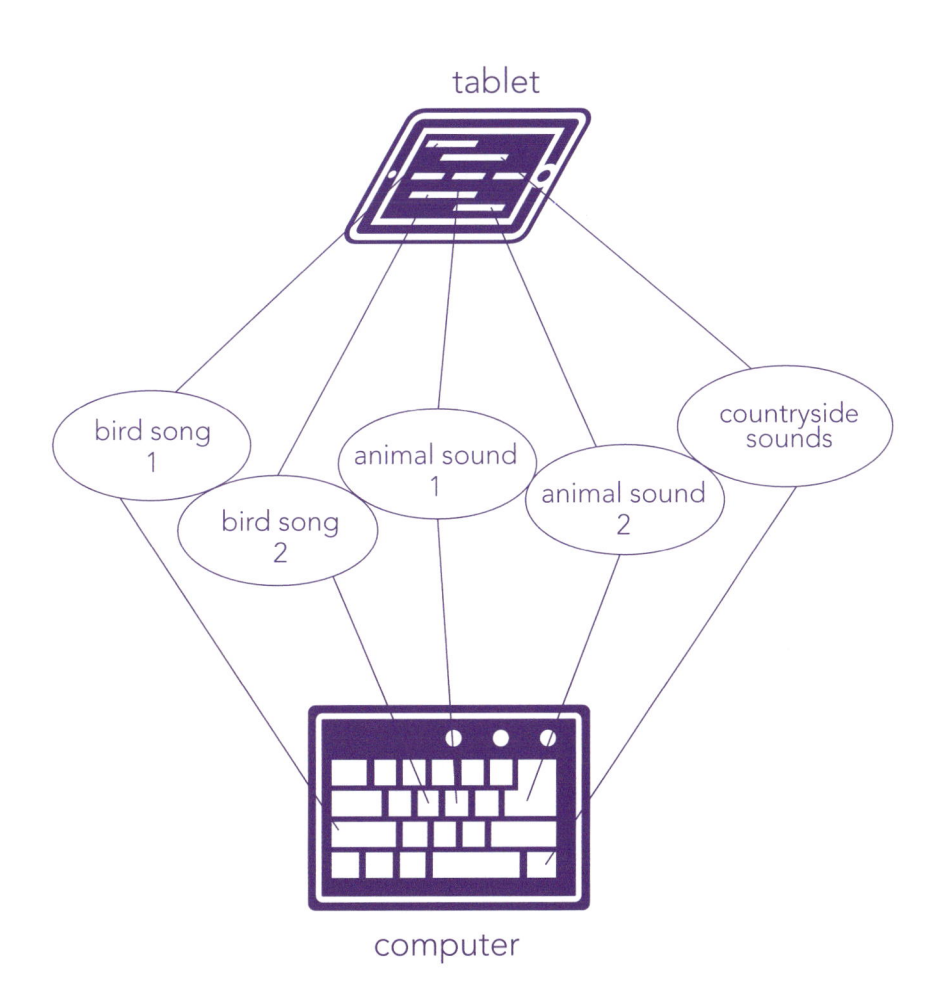

tablet

- bird song 1
- bird song 2
- animal sound 1
- animal sound 2
- countryside sounds

computer

Music-Makers

During the verses

Support participants in singing or playing the tune on a melody instrument (such as a keyboard or recorder). They may be able to play the bass line on a keyboard or bass guitar, and/or the chords on a keyboard, guitar or ukulele, using simpler versions (in bold) if preferred.

keys recorder bass guitar ukulele

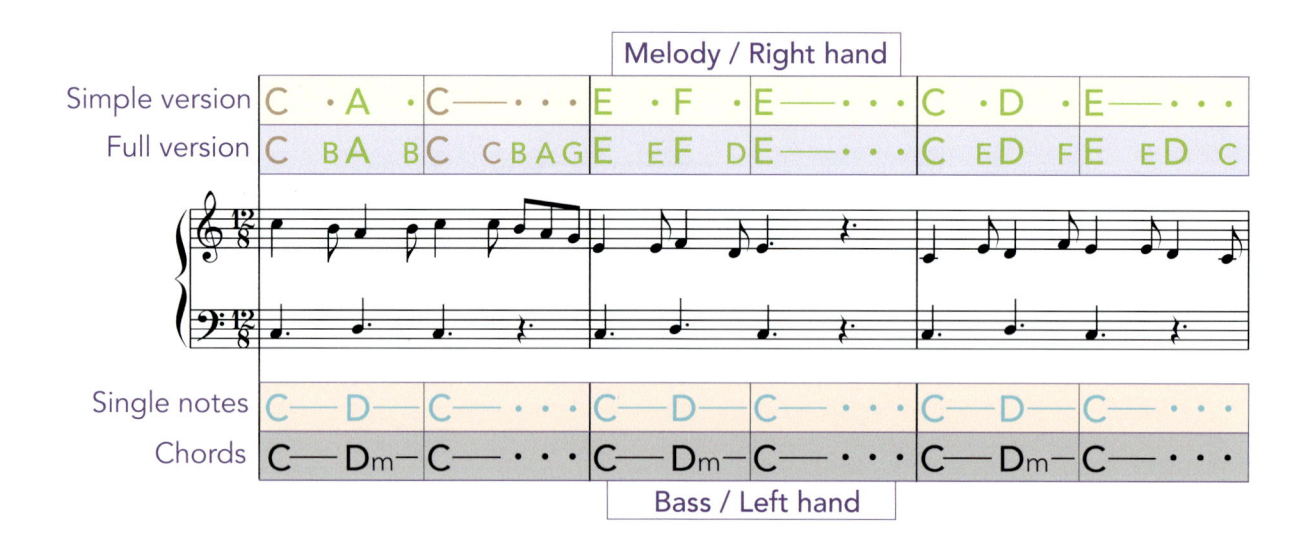

Melody / Right hand

Simple version	C · A · C — · · · ·	E · F · E — · · · ·	C · D · E — · · · ·
Full version	C BA BC CBAG	E EF DE — · · ·	C ED FE ED C

Single notes	C — D — C — · · ·	C — D — C — · · ·	C — D — C — · · ·
Chords	C — Dm — C — · · ·	C — Dm — C — · · ·	C — Dm — C — · · ·

Bass / Left hand

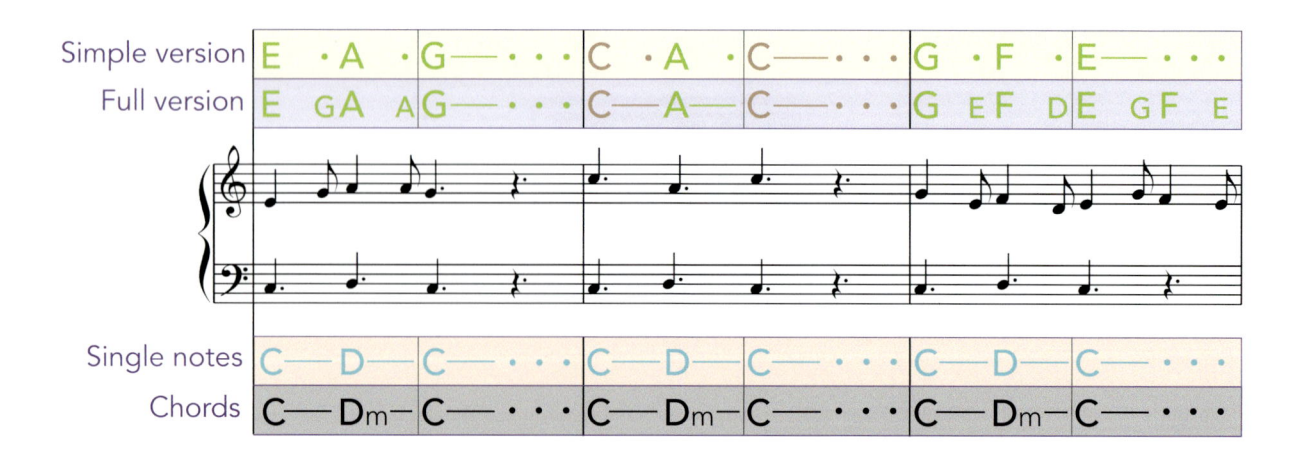

Simple version	E · A · G — · · · ·	C · A · C — · · · ·	G · F · E — · · · ·
Full version	E GA aG — · · ·	C — A — C — · · ·	G EF DE GF E

Single notes	C — D — C — · · ·	C — D — C — · · ·	C — D — C — · · ·
Chords	C — Dm — C — · · ·	C — Dm — C — · · ·	C — Dm — C — · · ·

Copyright material from Ockelford, Gray, Cohen and Mai (2023), *Count Me In!*, Routledge

ig

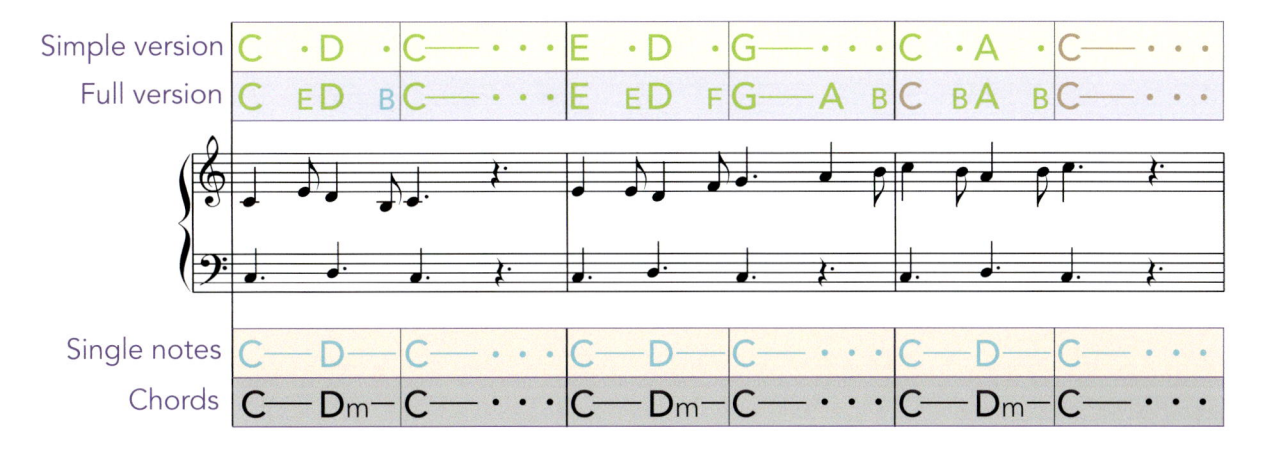

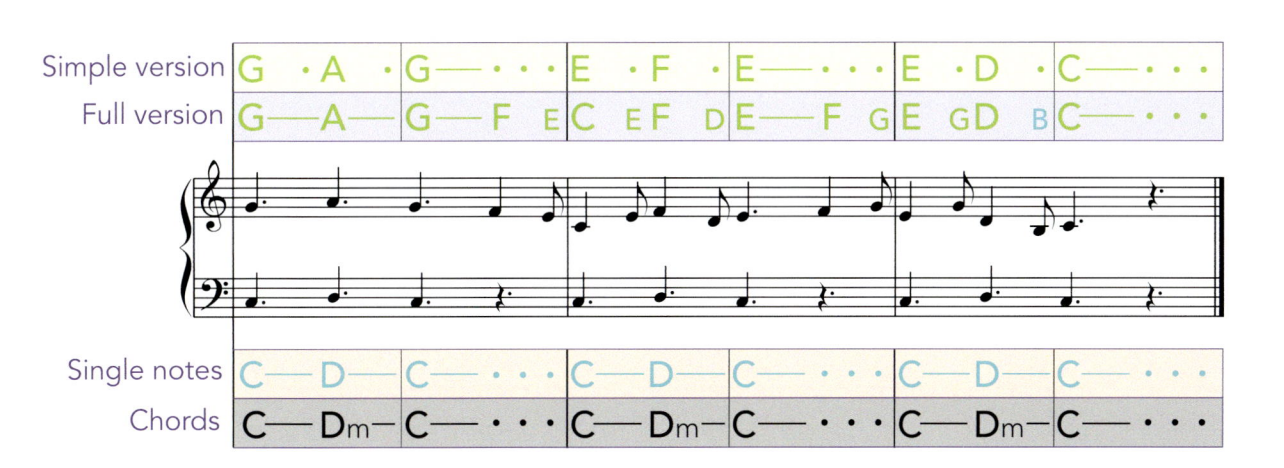

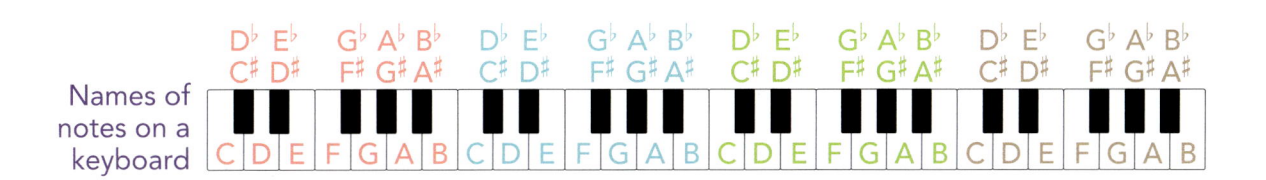

Summer

Score for music teachers to use

ig

Introduction

Water Blues is a song about water as we experience it in everyday life: falling as rain, dripping from a tap, overflowing from a flooded river and as the main constituent of our bodies. The song is in the style of the blues, which originated in the deep south of the United States at the end of the nineteenth century as a part of the African-American culture that was emerging there. During the twentieth century, the blues style influenced many other genres of music, including jazz, rock and roll, and pop.

Water Blues has four verses, each with parts for sound-makers, pattern-makers, motif-makers and music-makers. This means that all participants, irrespective of their capacity to engage with music, can join in together. After every verse there are improvised sections, each intended for players and singers at particular stages of musical development. The first is for sound-makers and is about rain. The second is for pattern-makers and concerns dripping taps. The third is for motif-makers and recreates the sounds of overflowing rivers. The fourth is for music-makers and has the sounds of bottles glugging and people slurping as they drink!

Musical resources required

Choose from the following according to participants' abilities, preferences and needs:

Sound-Makers

- Rainstick(s), ocean drum(s)
- Control of digitally recorded rain sounds through
    - gesture recognition technology (tablets/beams)
    - eye gaze technology
    - switch(es)

  that are loaded with sound files from https://www.soundsofintent.app/count-me-in
- Microphone(s) and amplifier(s), potentially with loop pedals and effects

Pattern-Makers

- Kalimba(s), also known as thumb piano(s), tongue drum(s)
- Pattern-making using individually recorded water drop sounds through
    - gesture recognition technology (tablets/beams)
    - eye gaze technology
    - switch(es)

  that are loaded with sound files from https://www.soundsofintent.app/count-me-in
- Microphone(s) and amplifier(s), potentially with loop pedals and effects unit(s)

Motif-Makers

- Wood block(s)
- Cabasa(s)
- Keyboard(s), recorder(s) and/or other wind instrument(s), tablet(s)
- Switch(es) loaded with a single cabasa sound
- Microphone(s) and amplifier(s), potentially with loop pedals and effects unit(s)

Music-Makers

- Keyboard(s), recorder(s) and/or other wind instrument(s), tablet(s)
- Guitar(s), ukulele(s), bass guitar(s)
- Microphone(s) and amplifier(s)

Additional items

Water Blues is suited very well to a multisensory approach – particularly for sound-makers and pattern-makers – and musical and other everyday sounds can be supplemented with bowls of water to splash hands and feet in, misters and other sprays, jugs for water to drip from and bottles half full of water that will glug when they are upended.

Strategies

If possible, listen to the piece a few times over a number of days before encouraging participants to join in. In this way, they may variously become familiar with the sounds, patterns, motifs, melodies and harmonies that are used. Remember that, in musical development, reactivity precedes interactivity and proactivity.

Individual parts can be practised one-to-one, and then in pairs or small groups, before you attempt to bring the whole texture together.

With each verse, using the backing track, start with sound-makers, then pattern-makers and motif-makers before song-makers come in with the main melody. The arrangements are suitable for participants at all levels of musical development. If some are not present or choose not to play or sing, the backing track will hold things together.

Links to other areas of experience and learning

In schools and colleges, *Water Blues* can link naturally to other areas of the curriculum, including health and well-being, science (chemistry and biology) and geography.

Water

Sound-Makers

During each verse

Encourage participants to play cascades of tinkling sounds freely throughout the verses, using bar chimes,

bar chimes

or by activating digitally recorded bar-chime sounds using gesture recognition technology such as that available on tablets and using beams,

beam

tablet

or switches or eye gaze technology to trigger pre-recorded cascades of bar-chime sounds.

switch 　　*eye gaze*

Introduction

↓

Verse 1
Water, water, everywhere,
It's pouring down with rain.
It pitters and patters all over the roof
And gurgles down the drain.
Water, water, everywhere,
It's pouring down with rain.

Verse 2
Water, water, everywhere,
Tap's dripping in the sink.
Turn it off real tight or there'll be
Nothing left to drink.
Water, water, everywhere,
Tap's dripping in the sink.

Verse 3
Water, water, everywhere,
The river has overflowed.
It's burst its banks and flooded the fields
And poured into the road.
Water, water, everywhere,
The river has overflowed.

Verse 4
Water, water, everywhere,
It's what we're mostly made of.
So don't run on empty, make sure you drink plenty,
There's nothing to be afraid of.
Water, water, everywhere,
It's what we're mostly made of.

Verse 4 (repeat)

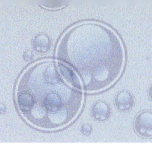

Sound-Makers

After Verse 1

Support participants to join in with the sounds of rain using a rainstick or an ocean drum,

rainstick  **ocean drum**

or trigger recorded rain sounds (from real life or created using musical instruments) using beams, tablets,

beam  **tablet**

switches or eye gaze technology.

switch  **eye gaze**

Participants may be able to vocalise rain-like sounds, which can be amplified and enhanced using effects such as reverberation, and repeated using a loop pedal.

mic

Sounds of rain pattering

Sounds of taps dripping

Sounds of river overflowing

Sounds of glugging

Copyright material from Ockelford, Gray, Cohen and Mai (2023), *Count Me In!*, Routledge

Water

Pattern-Makers

During each verse

Assist participants to join in with the regular beats in the song on the drum and cowbell. The drum is slow and the cowbell is twice the speed.

bang — bang
drum

tap — tap — tap — tap
cowbell

The sounds of the drum and cowbell can also be triggered using beams, tablets, switches or eye gaze technology.

- beam
- tablet
- switch
- eye gaze

Introduction
↓

Verse 1
Water, water, everywhere,
It's pouring down with rain.
It pitters and patters all over the roof
And gurgles down the drain.
Water, water, everywhere,
It's pouring down with rain.

Verse 2
Water, water, everywhere,
Tap's dripping in the sink.
Turn it off real tight or there'll be
Nothing left to drink.
Water, water, everywhere,
Tap's dripping in the sink.

Verse 3
Water, water, everywhere,
The river has overflowed.
It's burst its banks and flooded the fields
And poured into the road.
Water, water, everywhere,
The river has overflowed.

Verse 4
Water, water, everywhere,
It's what we're mostly made of.
So don't run on empty, make sure you drink plenty,
There's nothing to be afraid of.
Water, water, everywhere,
It's what we're mostly made of.

Verse 4 (repeat)

Copyright material from Ockelford, Gray, Cohen and Mai (2023), *Count Me In!*, Routledge

Blues

Pattern-Makers

After Verse 2

Show participants how to join in with the sound of a tap dripping using a kalimba (thumb piano)

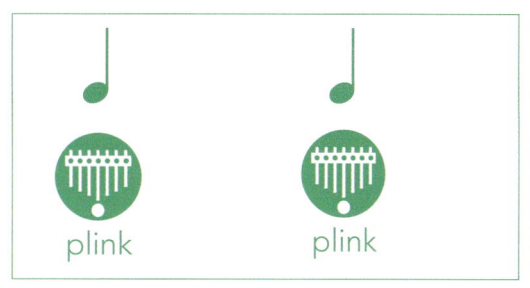

Sounds of rain pattering

plink   plink

kalimba

or a metal tongue drum.

Sounds of taps dripping

Encourage them to trigger single dripping sounds (from real life or created using musical instruments) using beams, tablets, switches or eye gaze technology, and repeat the sounds to make patterns. For example:

Sounds of river overflowing

slow repeated dripping sounds

switch

Help them to make patterns of dripping sounds using a microphone.

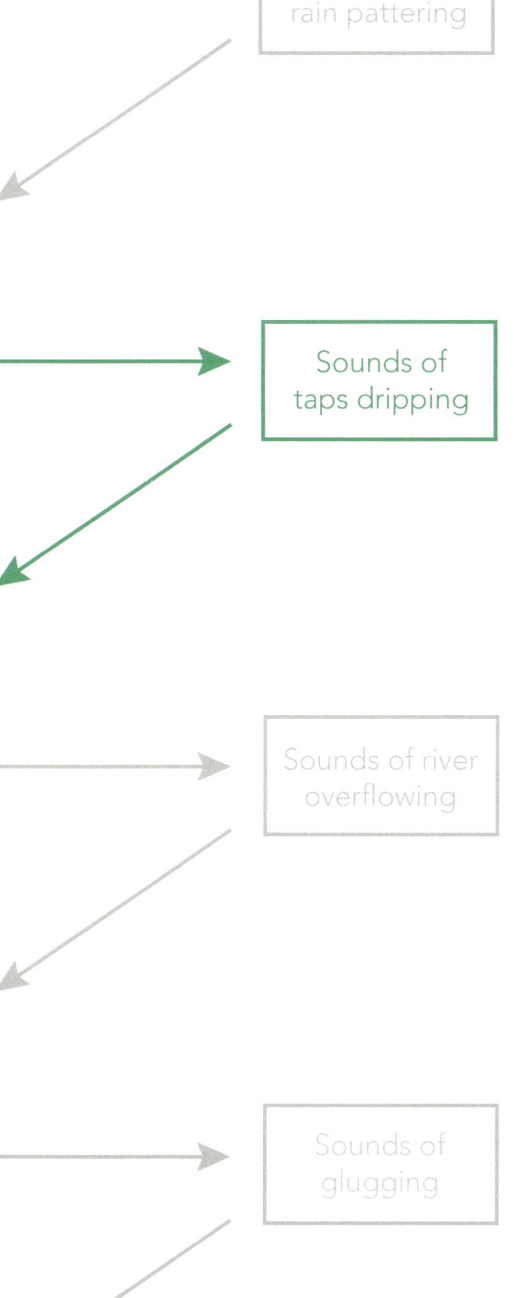

Sounds of glugging

quicker repeated dripping sounds

mic

Wate[r]

Motif-Makers

During each verse

Show participants how to join in with the groove of the piece with short bursts of rhythm on a wood block. To help keep the rhythm on track, try thinking of words that will fit. For example:

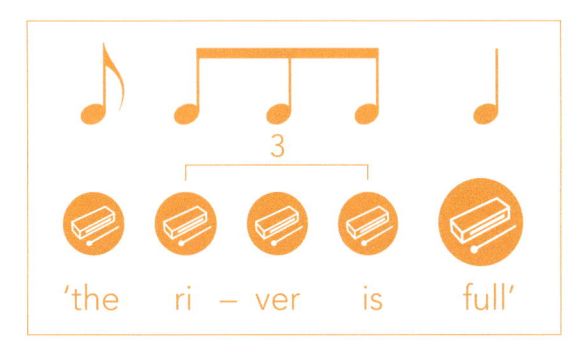

'the   ri – ver   is   full'

wood block

Using the same rhythm, teach participants to play a four-note riff on B, D and E. You could use a keyboard,

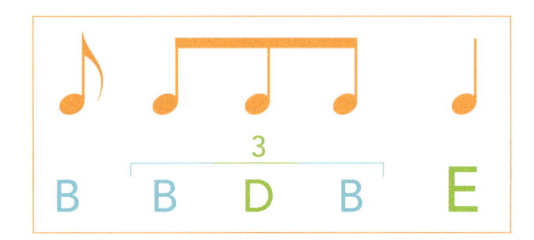

B B D B E

keys

or a wind instrument such as the recorder, or a tablet, or by singing (using a microphone if wished).

recorder   tablet   mic

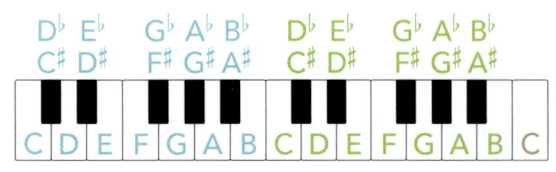

Names of notes on a keyboard

Introduction

↓

Verse 1
Water, water, everywhere,
It's pouring down with rain.
It pitters and patters all over the roof
And gurgles down the drain.
Water, water, everywhere,
It's pouring down with rain.

Verse 2
Water, water, everywhere,
Tap's dripping in the sink.
Turn it off real tight or there'll be
Nothing left to drink.
Water, water, everywhere,
Tap's dripping in the sink.

Verse 3
Water, water, everywhere,
The river has overflowed.
It's burst its banks and flooded the fields
And poured into the road.
Water, water, everywhere,
The river has overflowed.

Verse 4
Water, water, everywhere,
It's what we're mostly made of.
So don't run on empty, make sure you drink plenty,
There's nothing to be afraid of.
Water, water, everywhere,
It's what we're mostly made of.

Verse 4 (repeat)

Copyright material from Ockelford, Gray, Cohen and Mai (2023), *Count Me In!*, Routledge

Blues

Motif-Makers

After Verse 3

Show participants how to join in with the sound of a river overflowing by making sounds on the cabasa that form motifs. It may be helpful to think of words that fit. For example:

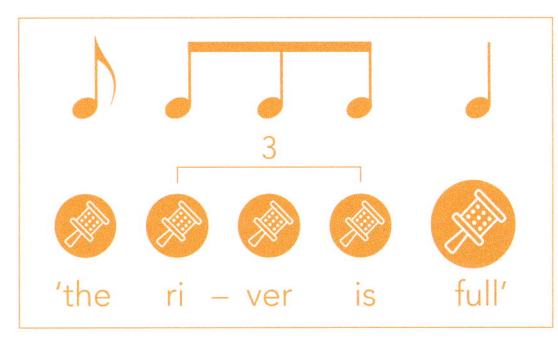

'the   ri – ver   is   full'

cabasa

Participants may be able to trigger a single sound of the cabasa using a switch, and then make motifs with repeated presses.

switch

Show them how to sing the phrase into a microphone (with words or non-verbal vocal sounds).

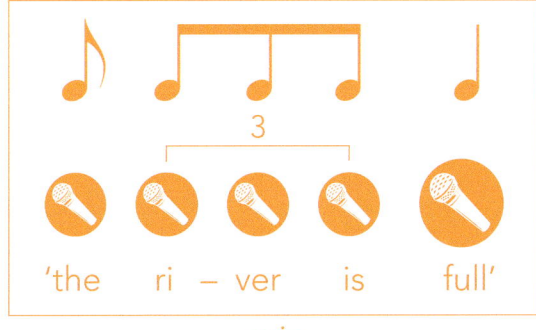

'the   ri – ver   is   full'

mic

Teach them how to play or sing the motif in patterns of 'call and response'.

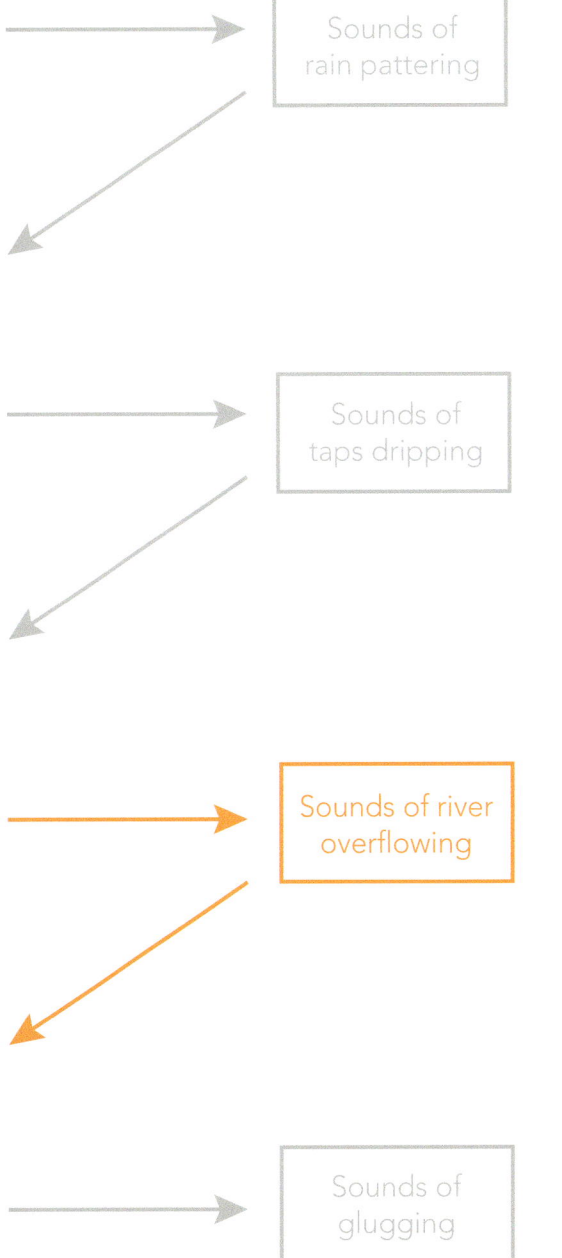

call

response

- Sounds of rain pattering
- Sounds of taps dripping
- **Sounds of river overflowing**
- Sounds of glugging

Copyright material from Ockelford, Gray, Cohen and Mai (2023), *Count Me In!*, Routledge

Water

Introduction

↓

Verse 1

Water, water, everywhere,
It's pouring down with rain.
It pitters and patters all over the roof
And gurgles down the drain.
Water, water, everywhere,
It's pouring down with rain.

→ Sounds of rain pattering

Verse 2

Water, water, everywhere,
Tap's dripping in the sink.
Turn it off real tight or there'll be
Nothing left to drink.
Water, water, everywhere,
Tap's dripping in the sink.

→ Sounds of taps dripping

Verse 3

Water, water, everywhere,
The river has overflowed.
It's burst its banks and flooded the fields
And poured into the road.
Water, water, everywhere,
The river has overflowed.

→ Sounds of river overflowing

Verse 4

Water, water, everywhere,
It's what we're mostly made of.
So don't run on empty, make sure you drink plenty,
There's nothing to be afraid of.
Water, water, everywhere,
It's what we're mostly made of.

→ Sounds of glugging

Verse 4 (repeat)

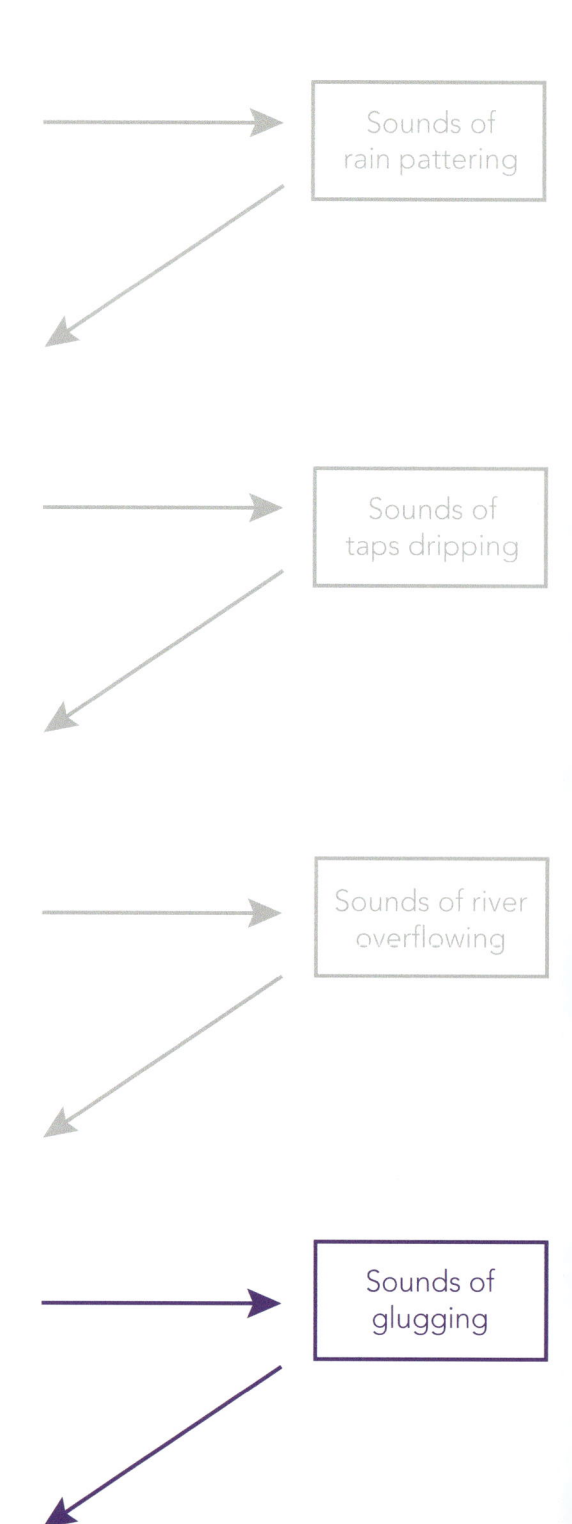

Blues

Music-Makers

During each verse and after Verse 4

Encourage participants to sing or play the tune on a melody instrument (such as a keyboard or recorder), show them how to play the bass line on a keyboard or bass guitar, or the chords on a keyboard, guitar or ukulele, using simpler versions (in bold) if preferred.

- keys
- recorder
- bass
- guitar
- ukulele

Melody / Right hand

Simple version	E	•	E	•	G	•	E	•	B	•	A	•	E	•	• •
Full version	E E	•	E E	•	G	E E	•	E	B	B♭	A	G	E	•	• E

Single notes	E	•	• •	A	•	G	•	E	•	• •	E	•	• •
Chords	E⁷	•	E⁷	•	A⁷	•	G⁶	•	E⁷	•	A⁹	•	E⁷	•	E⁷	•

Bass / Left hand

Simple version	E	•	E	•	G	•	E	•	B	•	A	•	E	•	• •
Full version	E E	• E	E	G	E	E	• E	B	B♭	A	G	E	•	• •

Single notes	A	•	• •	G	•	• •	F♯	•	G	•	G♯	•	G♮	•
Chords	A⁷	•	A⁷	•	G¹³	•	G¹³	•	F♯sus4	F♯	A⁷	•	G♯	•	G⁷	•

Simple version	B	•	B	•	D	•	B	•	B	•	A	•	E	•	• •
Full version	B B	•	B B	•	D	B B	•	B	B	B♭	A	G	E	•	• •

Single notes	F♯	•	• •	F	•	• •	E	•	• •	E	•	• •
Chords	B⁷sus4	•	B⁷	•	F¹³	•	F¹³	•	E⁷	•	A⁹	•	E⁷	• • •

Names of notes on a keyboard

Copyright material from Ockelford, Gray, Cohen and Mai (2023), *Count Me In!*, Routledge

Water

Score for music teachers to use

Voice / Keyboard

Wa-ter, wa-ter,

1. ev–'ry-where, It's pour-ing down with rain. It pitters and patters all over the roof and
2. ev–'ry-where, Tap's drip-ping in the sink. Turn it off real tight or there'll be
3. ev–'ry-where, The river has ov–er–flowed. It's burst its banks and flooded the fields and
4. ev–'ry-where, It's what we're most-ly made of. So don't run on empty make sure you drink plenty, then

1. gur–gles down the drain. Wa-ter, wa-ter, ev–'ry-where, It's pour-ing down with rain.
2. no–thing left to drink. Wa-ter, wa-ter, ev–'ry-where, Tap's drip-ping in the sink.
3. poured in-to the road. Wa-ter, wa-ter, ev–'ry-where, The river has ov–er–flowed
4. nothing to be a–fraid of. Wa-ter, wa-ter, ev–'ry-where, It's what we're most-ly made

Copyright material from Ockelford, Gray, Cohen and Mai (2023), *Count Me In!*, Routledge

Blues

Young people with profound disabilities enjoy making water-like sounds

Rainbow

Introduction

Rainbow Rag combines two lines of thought. First, it sets out the seven colours of the rainbow: red, orange, yellow, green, blue, indigo and violet. Second, it compares this spectrum with human diversity, in which everyone is different, but all people are essential to and of equal value in an inclusive society. The song is in the style of ragtime, which was popularised in the early twentieth century by the American composer and pianist, Scott Joplin. It was called 'ragtime' because of its 'ragged' or syncopated rhythms. The best know rag is *The Entertainer,* which was used in the film *The Sting* and more recently in the video game *Gran Turismo 5.*

Rainbow Rag has two stanzas, which are repeated, making four verses in all. Each has parts for sound-makers, pattern-makers, motif-makers and music-makers. So all participants, no matter what their level of musical development, can join in together. Between verses there are improvised sections, each intended for players and singers who are able to engage with music in different ways. The first is for sound-makers, the second for pattern-makers, the third for motif-makers, and the fourth for music-makers.

Musical resources required

Choose from the following, according to participants' abilities, preferences and needs:

Sound-Makers

- Triangle(s), tambourine(s)
- Control of digitally recorded triangle, tambourine and honky-tonk piano sounds through
    - gesture recognition technology (tablets/beams)
    - eye gaze technology
    - switch(es)

   that are loaded with sound files from https://www.soundsofintent.app/count-me-in
- Microphone(s) and amplifier(s), potentially with loop pedal and effects

Pattern-Makers

- Drum(s), wood block(s), claves
- Pattern-making through individually recorded percussive sounds using a switch or switches that are loaded with sound files from https://www.soundsofintent.app/count-me-in

Motif-Makers

- Cabasa(s), drums of two different sizes
- Keyboard(s), recorder(s) and/or other wind instrument(s)
- Microphone(s) and amplifier(s)

Music-Makers

- Keyboard(s), recorder(s) and/or other wind instrument(s), tablet(s)
- Guitar(s), ukulele(s), bass guitar(s)
- Microphone(s) and amplifier(s)

Additional items

Rainbow Rag can be performed in a multisensory way, with streamers, sashes, ribbons or veils of different colours, and/or coloured lights. Participants could dress in different colours.

Strategies

If possible, listen to *Rainbow Rag* a few times over a number of days before encouraging participants to join in. In this way they may become familiar with the sounds, patterns, motifs, melodies and harmonies that are used. It is important to remember that, in musical development (as in aural traditions), listening precedes active participation.

Individual parts can be practised one-to-one, and then in pairs or small groups, before attempting to bring the whole texture together.

With each verse, using the backing track, start with sound-makers, then pattern-makers and motif-makers before encouraging music-makers to come in with the main melody. The arrangements are suitable for participants playing and singing in groups, large and small. If some are not present or choose not to play or sing, the backing track will hold things together.

Links to other areas of experience and learning

In schools and colleges, *Rainbow Rag* has potential links to other curricular areas, such as science (physics), geography (the weather) and citizenship (awareness of others, difference, diversity and human rights).

Rainbow

Sound-Makers

During each verse

Encourage participants to shake the tambourine from time to time.

tambourine

Help them ding the triangle now and then.

triangle

Or support them in making similar sounds by activating digitally recorded tambourine or triangle sounds using gesture recognition technology such as that available on tablets and using beams,

beam   **tablet**

or by using switches or eye gaze technology.

switch   **eye gaze**

Introduction
Sound-makers only

↓

Verse 1
Instruments only

Verse 2
Red and orange and yellow and green,
Blue, indigo and violet.
These are colours that can be seen,
When raindrops are sunlit.

Red and orange and yellow and green,
Blue, indigo and violet.
These are colours that can be seen,
In a rainbow.

Verse 3
We are different, you and me,
And everyone else, wherever they may be.
But we're all people equally,
Living together.

We are different, you and me,
And everyone else, wherever they may be.
But we're all people equally,
In the human rainbow.

Verse 4
Repeat Verse 3 with the new melody too

Copyright material from Ockelford, Gray, Cohen and Mai (2023), *Count Me In!*, Routledge

Rag

Sweeps of notes using honky-tonk piano sounds

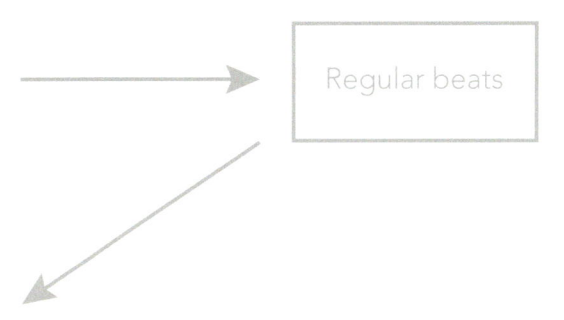

Regular beats

Melodic and rhythmic motifs

New melody with the same harmonies

Sound-Makers

In the Introduction

Show participants how to trigger pre-recorded honky-tonk piano sounds using a switch or eye gaze technology,

switch

eye gaze

or help them play sweeping sounds using a beam or tablet loaded with honky-tonk piano sounds,

tablet

beam

or on a keyboard.

keys

Copyright material from Ockelford, Gray, Cohen and Mai (2023), *Count Me In!*, Routledge

Rainbow

Pattern-Makers

During each verse

Assist participants in joining in with the regular beats in the song on the drum and the woodblock. The drum is 'on the beat', and the wood block is 'off the beat'. It can be difficult to play off the beat to start with, and it may help to play the instruments alternately, left hand, right hand, and so on.

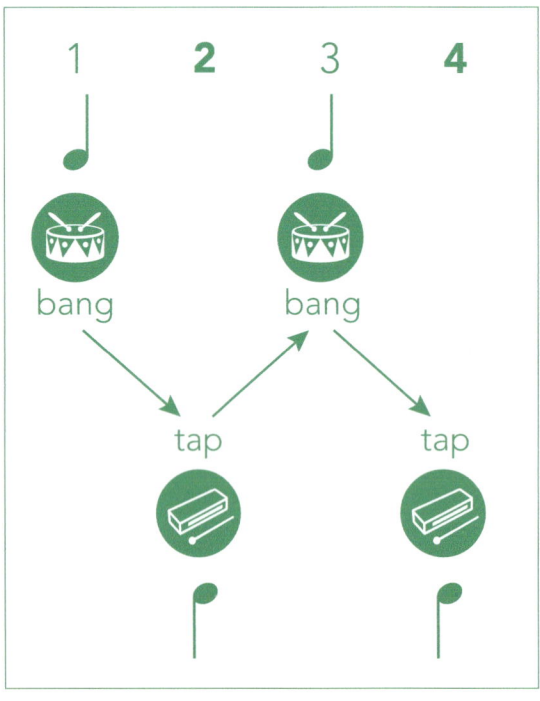

1 2 3 4

bang — bang
tap — tap

drum and wood block

Then have them try the wood block on its own.

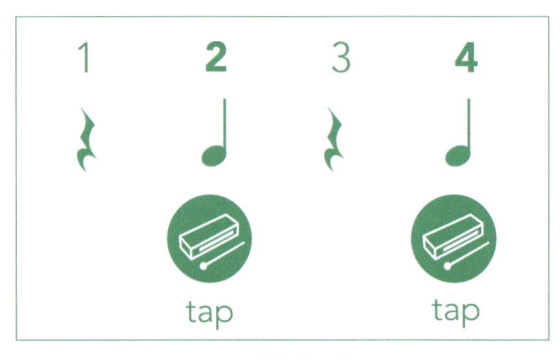

1 2 3 4

tap — tap

wood block

Introduction
Sound-makers only

↓

Verse 1
Instruments only

Verse 2
Red and orange and yellow and green,
Blue, indigo and violet.
These are colours that can be seen,
When raindrops are sunlit.

Red and orange and yellow and green,
Blue, indigo and violet.
These are colours that can be seen,
In a rainbow.

Verse 3
We are different, you and me,
And everyone else, wherever they may be.
But we're all people equally,
Living together.

We are different, you and me,
And everyone else, wherever they may be.
But we're all people equally,
In the human rainbow.

Verse 4
Repeat Verses 2 and 3

Copyright material from Ockelford, Gray, Cohen and Mai (2023), *Count Me In!*, Routledge

Rag

Sweeps of notes using honky-tonk piano sounds

Regular beats

Melodic and rhythmic motifs

New melody with the same harmonies

Pattern-Makers

After Verse 2

Show participants how to improvise new beats to add to those in the backing track: fast and slow, loud and quiet, on different instruments, some with many repetitions and some with few. For example:

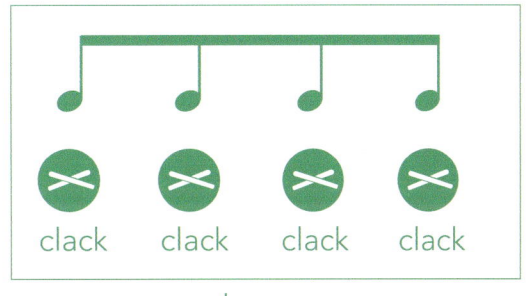

clack   clack   clack   clack

at a moderate speed and fairly loudly

claves

slowly and loudly

drum

quickly and quietly

woodblock

very slowly and very loudly

switch linked to cymbal

Copyright material from Ockelford, Gray, Cohen and Mai (2023), *Count Me In!*, Routledge

Rainbow

Motif-Makers

During each verse

Show participants how to join in with the groove of the piece with short bursts of rhythm on a cabasa. To help them keep the rhythm on track, try thinking of words that fit. For example:

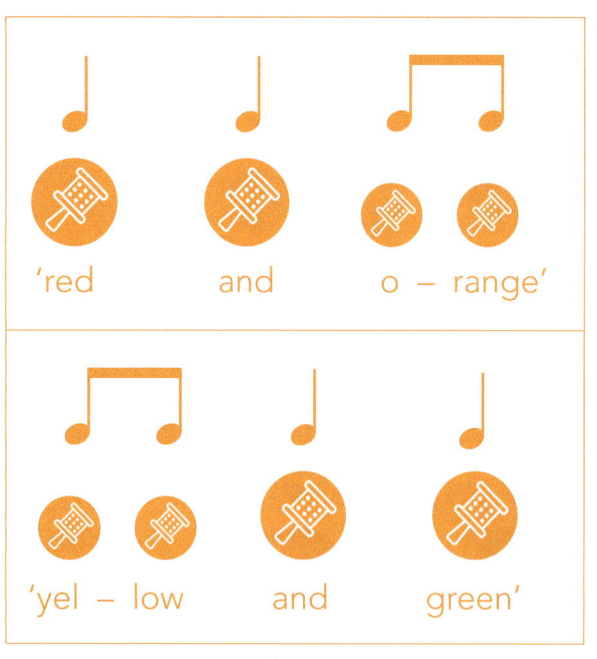

'red   and   o – range'

'yel – low   and   green'

cabasa

Teach them how to play the rhythms on two instruments, by using drums of different sizes, for example.

bang bang bang boom

drums

Introduction
Sound-makers only

↓

Verse 1
Instruments only

Verse 2
Red and orange and yellow and green,
Blue, indigo and violet.
These are colours that can be seen,
When raindrops are sunlit.

Red and orange and yellow and green,
Blue, indigo and violet.
These are colours that can be seen,
In a rainbow.

Verse 3
We are different, you and me,
And everyone else, wherever they may be.
But we're all people equally,
Living together.

We are different, you and me,
And everyone else, wherever they may be.
But we're all people equally,
In the human rainbow.

Verse 4
Repeat Verses 2 and 3

Copyright material from Ockelford, Gray, Cohen and Mai (2023), *Count Me In!*, Routledge

Rag

Sweeps of notes using honky-tonk piano sounds

Regular beats

Melodic and rhythmic motifs

New melody with the same harmonies

Motif-Makers

After Verse 3

Model 'question and answer' activities to the backing track. You could use short rhythms or fragments of melody from the song, sung or played. For example:

QUESTION

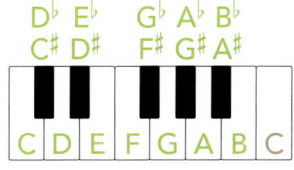

C	E	G G
'red	and	o – range'

mic or keys or recorder

ANSWER

F F	E	D
'yel – low	and	green'

mic or keys or recorder

D♭ E♭   G♭ A♭ B♭
C♯ D♯   F♯ G♯ A♯
C D E F G A B C

Names of notes on a keyboard

Copyright material from Ockelford, Gray, Cohen and Mai (2023), *Count Me In!*, Routledge

Rainbow

Introduction — Sound-makers only → Sweeps of notes using honky-tonk piano sounds

Verse 1 — Instruments only → Regular beats

Verse 2

Red and orange and yellow and green,
Blue, indigo and violet.
These are colours that can be seen,
When raindrops are sunlit.

Red and orange and yellow and green,
Blue, indigo and violet.
These are colours that can be seen,
In a rainbow.

→ Melodic and rhythmic motifs

Verse 3

We are different, you and me,
And everyone else, wherever they may be.
But we're all people equally,
Living together.

We are different, you and me,
And everyone else, wherever they may be.
But we're all people equally,
In the human rainbow.

→ New melody with the same harmonies

Verse 4 — Repeat Verse 3 with the new melody too

Music-Makers

During each verse

Show participants how to sing or play the tune on a melody instrument (such as a keyboard or recorder), and/or the bass line on a keyboard or bass guitar. Teach them how to play the chords on a keyboard, guitar or ukulele, using simpler versions (in bold) if preferred.

- mic
- keys
- recorder
- bass
- guitar
- ukulele

First time play this line

Second time play this line

Repeat from the beginning

Play the whole thing again

Copyright material from Ockelford, Gray, Cohen and Mai (2023), *Count Me In!*, Routledge

Rainbow

Music-Makers

After Verse 3

Encourage participants to sing or play the tune on a melody instrument (such as a keyboard or recorder), and/or to play the bass line on a keyboard or bass guitar. Help them to play the chords on a keyboard, guitar or ukulele, using simpler versions (in bold) if preferred.

- keys
- recorder
- bass
- guitar
- ukulele

Melody / Right hand

Additional tune	E	—	D	C	D	—	D	—	F	—	E	D	E	—	E
Original tune	C	E	G	G	F	F	E	D	—	B	D	F F F F	E	D	C —

Lyrics:
1. Look at the rain-bow, Look at the rain-bow,
2. Look all a-round you, Look all a-round you,

Single notes	C —	E	G —	B —	G —	A	B	C	B	C —
Chords	C —	C —	G⁷ —	G⁷ —	G⁷ —	G⁷ —	C —	C —

Bass / Left hand

Names of notes on a keyboard: C D E F G A B (repeated across octaves, with black keys C♯/D♭, D♯/E♭, F♯/G♭, G♯/A♭, A♯/B♭)

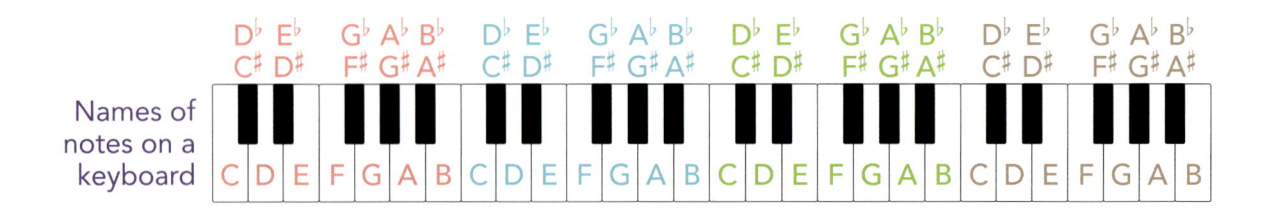

Copyright material from Ockelford, Gray, Cohen and Mai (2023), *Count Me In!*, Routledge

Rag

First time play this line

Additional tune	F	E	D	G	G	F♯	G	
Original tune	A A	G G C	D C	B — B	A	A B	G	G

1. See its co – lours shin – ing bright.
2. We're all peo – ple e – qual – ly.

Repeat from the beginning

Single notes	F	C D E	F♯ D	G	D	D	G F	E D
Chords	F	C	D⁷	G	Dsus4	D	G	G

Second time play this line

Additional tune	F	E	D	C	G	G	G	C ·
Original tune	A A	G♯ G♯ G	F♯ F	E E F	G G♭	F E	E♭ D	C ·

1. See its co – lours in the sun – light.
2. We're all e – qual mus – i – cal – ly.

Play the whole thing again

Single notes	C	B	A	G	G	A	B	C ·
Chords	F	E Em	D Dm	C	G	G⁷	G G⁷	C ·

Rainbow

Score for music teachers to use

1. Red and o-range and yel-low and green,
   Blue_____ in-di-go and vi - o - let. These are
   co-lours that can be seen, when rain - drops are

2. We are diff-'rent, you and me and
   every - one else where - ever they may be. But we're all
   peo - ple e - qual - ly, liv - ing to -

Rag

D.C. al Coda

| G | G7 | G | | | G7 |

1. sun — lit.
2. geth — er.

| F | E7 | A7 | D7 | G7 | C |

1. These are co-lours that can be seen in a
2. we're all peo — ple e — qual — ly, in the

| Em | E♭m | Dm | C#m | D7♭9 | G7 | C |

1. rain_____ bow.
2. hu_____ man rain_____ bow.

Copyright material from Ockelford, Gray, Cohen and Mai (2023), *Count Me In!*, Routledge

Introduction

Urban Rap is written in hip-hop style, in which words are chanted rhythmically over a beat. Hip-hop emerged in the 1970s from among the African American, Caribbean American and Latino American communities living in the Bronx, New York City.

Most raps are inspired by real life situations that the performer has experienced. *Urban Rap* is written from the imaginary perspective of a young person who lives in a city and reflects on the everyday sounds that pervade the environment where they live. Verse 1 describes the noises of traffic that intrude, day and night; Verse 2 speaks of the roar of jet engines as planes come in to land at a nearby airport; Verse 3 gives an account of the sirens of emergency vehicles; Verse 4 tells of the sounds that joggers make as they run by; Verse 5 is about bikes and trikes; and Verse 6 conjures up the sounds of people, laughing and chatting as they walk along. It is these – human – sounds that make the rapper feel at home.

During the verses, different parts are provided for sound-makers, pattern-makers, motif-makers and music-makers. After each verse, there are opportunities for sound-makers, pattern-makers and motif-makers to create their own soundscapes, using the resources available on the *Count Me In!* website, or their own pre-recorded sounds.

Musical resources required

Choose from the following, according to participants' abilities, preferences and needs:

Sound-Makers

- Control of digitally recorded urban sounds, including the jet engines of aeroplanes and whirring bike chains, through
    - gesture recognition technology (tablets/beams)
    - eye gaze technology
    - switch(es)

    that are loaded with sound files from https://www.soundsofintent.app/count-me-in

Pattern-Makers

- Drum(s), wood block(s), hi-hat(s)
- Digitally recorded individual toots on car horns and joggers' footsteps, triggered through
    - switch(es) or tablet(s)

    that are loaded with sound files from https://www.soundsofintent.app/count-me-in

Motif-Makers

- Two drums of different sizes
- Keyboard(s), recorder(s), ocarina(s), glockenspiel(s)

- Individual pitches, three notes apart (such as G and E) triggered through a switch or switch(es) or using tablet(s) that are loaded with sound files from https://www.soundsofintent.app/count-me-in
- Microphone(s) and amplifier(s)

Music-Makers

- Bass guitar(s), keyboard(s)
- Microphone(s) and amplifier(s)

Additional items

The musical ideas underlying *Urban Rap* can be introduced as part of a wider presentation of hip-hop culture, and *Urban Rap* lends itself well to multisensory work, with the possibility of a different visual scene being shown to illustrate the content of each verse, and items such as bicycle bells and trainers being handed around at the appropriate points.

Strategies

Aim for participants to hear *Urban Rap* several times before attempting sessions in which they are asked to make music themselves. In this way they may become familiar with the sounds, patterns, motifs, melodies and harmonies that are used. This approach mirrors the usual pattern of musical development, in which listening and observation occur before attempts at joining in.

Each participant's part can be practised individually, and then with one or two other people, before an attempt is made to perform the piece as a whole.

Links to other areas of experience and learning

In schools and colleges, *Urban Rap* has potential links to other areas of the curriculum, including history (the emergence of rap in 1970s America and its relationship to wider political and cultural movements) and geography (the impact of noise pollution on city dwellers).

Sound-Makers

During each verse

Help participants activate digitally recorded urban street sounds at any point using gesture recognition technology such as that available on tablets and using beams,

- tablet
- beam

or by using switches or eye gaze technology.

- switch
- eye gaze

Verse 1
On the street where I live
There are cars drivin' by,
Tootin' their horns all day and night.
Revvin' their engines and steppin' on the brakes.
I can't sleep for the noise they make.

Verse 2
On the street where I live
There are planes overhead,
Comin' into Heathrow, my daddy said.
The roar of the engines gets in my head.
Have to shut the window when I go to bed.

Verse 3
On the street where I live
The sirens whine,
Nee-naw, nee-naw, all the time.
Police cars, fire engines, ambulances, more …
I'm glad it's not me they're comin' for.

Verse 4
On the street where I live
There are joggers joggin' through,
Sweatin' in their lycra and their Nike trainin' shoes.
A-huffin' and a-puffin' as they get in the flow.
It makes me feel tired just to watch them go.

Verse 5
On the street where I live
There are people ridin' bikes:
Carbon fibre racers and little kids' trikes.
Some you have to pedal and some you just sit,
Relyin' on the batt'ry to do its bit.

Verse 6
On the street where I live
There are people walkin' by,
A-laughin' and a-joshin' and sayin' 'hi'.
Sometimes they stop and talk to me
On my street – there's no place I'd rather be.

Rap

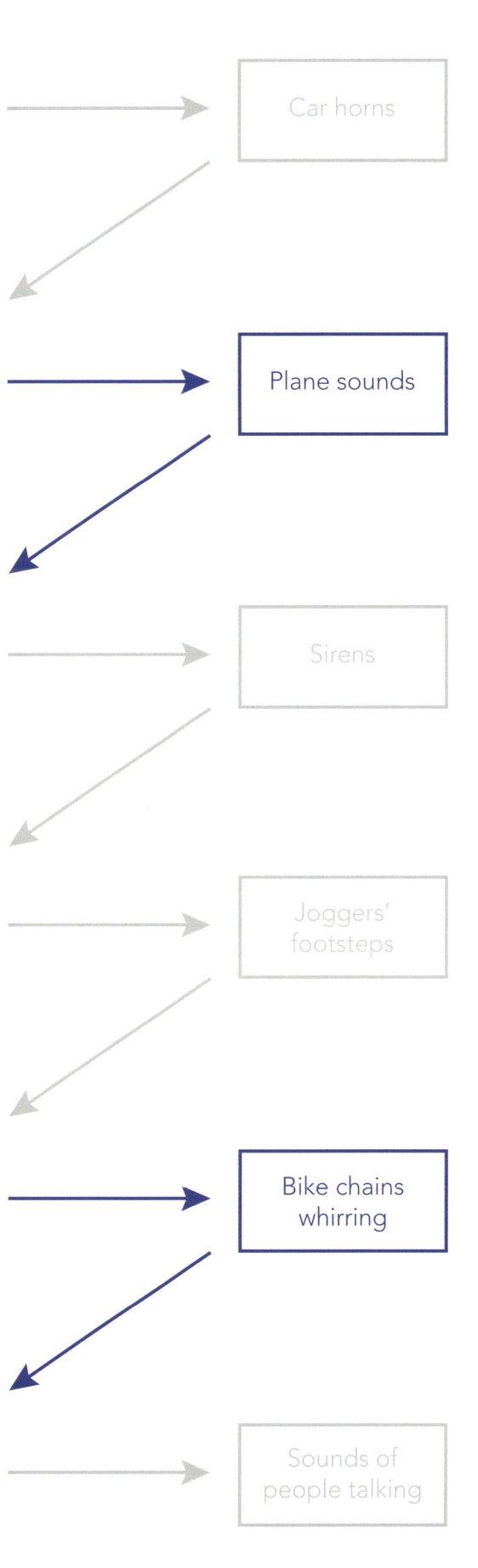

Car horns	
Plane sounds	
Sirens	
Joggers' footsteps	
Bike chains whirring	
Sounds of people talking	

Sound-Makers

After Verse 2

Enable participants to trigger the sounds of aeroplanes using gesture recognition technology such as that available on tablets and using beams, or by using switches or eye gaze devices.

- tablet
- beam
- switch
- eye gaze

After Verse 5

Help participants trigger the sounds of bike chains whirring using gesture recognition technology such as that available on tablets and using beams, or by using switches or eye gaze devices.

- tablet
- beam
- switch
- eye gaze

Copyright material from Ockelford, Gray, Cohen and Mai (2023), *Count Me In!*, Routledge

Pattern-Makers

During each verse

Show participants how to join in the regular beat of the song by clapping or striking a drum, wood block or a closed hi-hat from a drum kit.

clap	clap	clap	clap
bang	bang	bang	bang
tap	tap	tap	tap
chick	chick	chick	chick

hands, drum, wood block, closed hi-hat

Verse 1
On the street where I live
There are cars driving by,
Tootin' their horns all day and night.
Revvin' their engines and steppin' on the brakes.
I can't sleep for the noise they make.

Verse 2
On the street where I live
There are planes overhead,
Comin' into Heathrow, my daddy said.
The roar of the engines gets in my head.
Have to shut the window when I go to bed.

Verse 3
On the street where I live
The sirens whine,
Nee-naw, nee-naw, all the time.
Police cars, fire engines, ambulances, more …
I'm glad it's not me they're comin' for.

Verse 4
On the street where I live
There are joggers joggin' through,
Sweatin' in their lycra and their Nike trainin' shoes.
A-huffin' and a-puffin' as they get in the flow.
It makes me feel tired just to watch them go.

Verse 5
On the street where I live
There are people ridin' bikes:
Carbon fibre racers and little kids' trikes.
Some you have to pedal and some you just sit,
Relyin' on the batt'ry to do its bit.

Verse 6
On the street where I live
There are people walkin' by,
A-laughin' and a-joshin' and sayin' 'hi'.
Sometimes they stop and talk to me
On my street – there's no place I'd rather be.

Copyright material from Ockelford, Gray, Cohen and Mai (2023), *Count Me In!*, Routledge

Rap

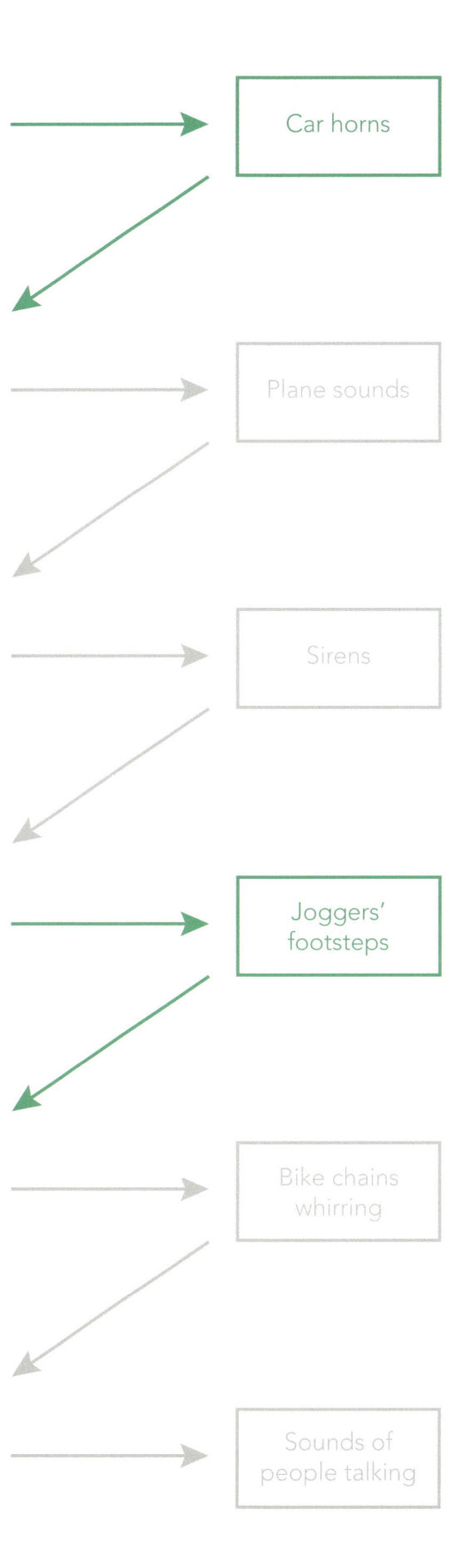

Pattern-Makers

After Verse 1

Teach participants how to make regular patterns at different speeds, using switches or tablets to activate digitally recorded sounds of individual toots on car horns.

Car horns

slower toots

tablet

more rapid toots

switch

After Verse 4

Show participants how to make regular patterns at different speeds, using switches or tablets to activate digitally recorded sounds of joggers' individual footsteps.

Plane sounds

Sirens

Joggers' footsteps

Bike chains whirring

Sounds of people talking

slower footsteps

tablet

more rapid footsteps

switch

Motif-Makers

During each verse

Encourage participants to join in with the groove of the piece with short bursts of rhythm on two different drums. To help keep the rhythm on track, try thinking of words that fit. For example:

| **1** | 2 | 3 | 4 | **1** | 2 | 3 | 4 |

boom — boom
bang — bang

'play   the   rhy – thm'

drums of different sizes

Verse 1
On the street where I live
There are cars driving by,
Tootin' their horns all day and night.
Revvin' their engines and steppin' on the brakes.
I can't sleep for the noise they make.

Verse 2
On the street where I live
There are planes overhead,
Comin' into Heathrow, my daddy said.
The roar of the engines gets in my head.
Have to shut the window when I go to bed.

Verse 3
On the street where I live
The sirens whine,
Nee-naw, nee-naw, all the time.
Police cars, fire engines, ambulances, more …
I'm glad it's not me they're comin' for.

Verse 4
On the street where I live
There are joggers joggin' through,
Sweatin' in their lycra and their Nike trainin' shoes.
A-huffin' and a-puffin' as they get in the flow.
It makes me feel tired just to watch them go.

Verse 5
On the street where I live
There are people ridin' bikes:
Carbon fibre racers and little kids' trikes.
Some you have to pedal and some you just sit,
Relyin' on the batt'ry to do its bit.

Verse 6
On the street where I live
There are people walkin' by,
A-laughin' and a-joshin' and sayin' 'hi'.
Sometimes they stop and talk to me
On my street – there's no place I'd rather be.

Copyright material from Ockelford, Gray, Cohen and Mai (2023), *Count Me In!*, Routledge

Rap

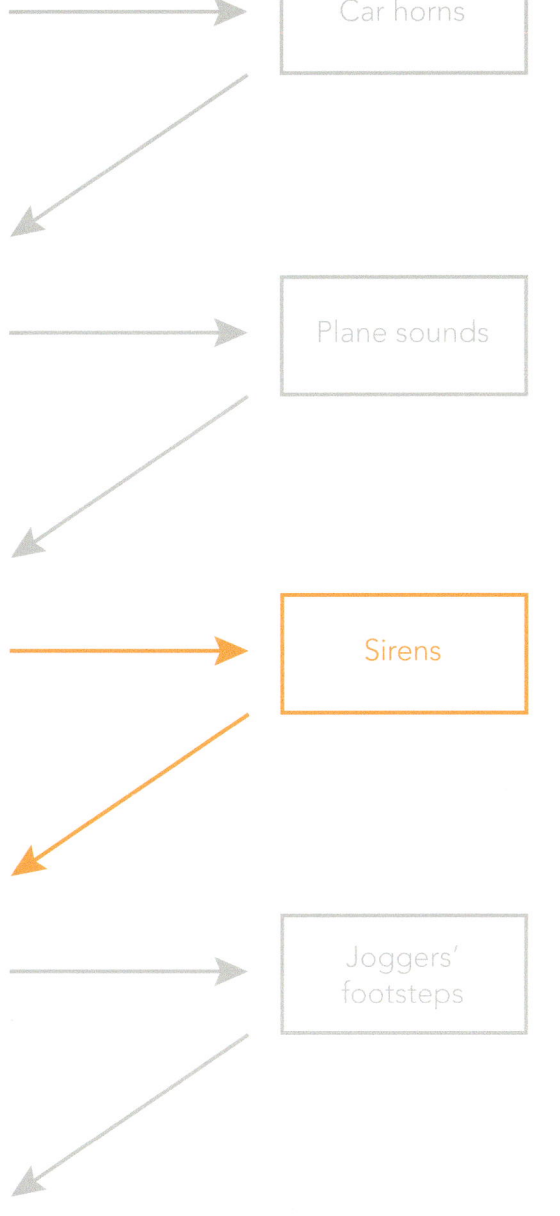

Motif-Makers

After Verse 3

Show participants how to make siren sounds using two alternating notes that are three letter names apart, like G and E, for example, on a melody instrument such as a keyboard, recorder, ocarina or glockenspiel,

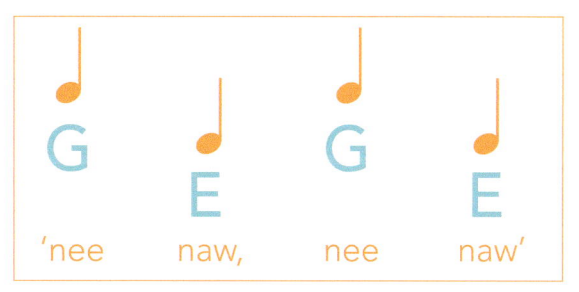

G	E	G	E
'nee	naw,	nee	naw'

keys   recorder   ocarina   glock

or by singing,

mic

or by using switches or gesture recognition technology such as that found on tablets or by using beams that trigger pre-recorded individual notes that, when played successively, make siren sounds.

tablet   switch

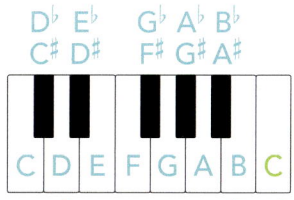

D♭ E♭   G♭ A♭ B♭
C♯ D♯   F♯ G♯ A♯

C D E F G A B C

Names of notes on a keyboard

Car horns →
Plane sounds →
Sirens →
Joggers' footsteps →
Bike chains whirring →
Sounds of people talking →

Copyright material from Ockelford, Gray, Cohen and Mai (2023), *Count Me In!*, Routledge

Urban

Verse 1
On the street where I live
There are cars driving by,
Tootin' their horns all day and night.
Revvin' their engines and steppin' on the brakes.
I can't sleep for the noise they make.

Car horns

Verse 2
On the street where I live
There are planes overhead,
Comin' into Heathrow, my daddy said.
The roar of the engines gets in my head.
Have to shut the window when I go to bed.

Plane sounds

Verse 3
On the street where I live
The sirens whine,
Nee-naw, nee-naw, all the time.
Police cars, fire engines, ambulances, more …
I'm glad it's not me they're comin' for.

Sirens

Verse 4
On the street where I live
There are joggers joggin' through,
Sweatin' in their lycra and their Nike trainin' shoes.
A-huffin' and a-puffin' as they get in the flow.
It makes me feel tired just to watch them go.

Joggers' footsteps

Verse 5
On the street where I live
There are people ridin' bikes:
Carbon fibre racers and little kids' trikes.
Some you have to pedal and some you just sit,
Relyin' on the batt'ry to do its bit.

Bike chains whirring

Verse 6
On the street where I live
There are people walkin' by,
A-laughin' and a-joshin' and sayin' 'hi'.
Sometimes they stop and talk to me
On my street – there's no place I'd rather be.

Sounds of people talking

Copyright material from Ockelford, Gray, Cohen and Mai (2023), *Count Me In!*, Routledge

Music-Makers

During each verse

Teach participants to play the bass line on a bass guitar or keyboard.

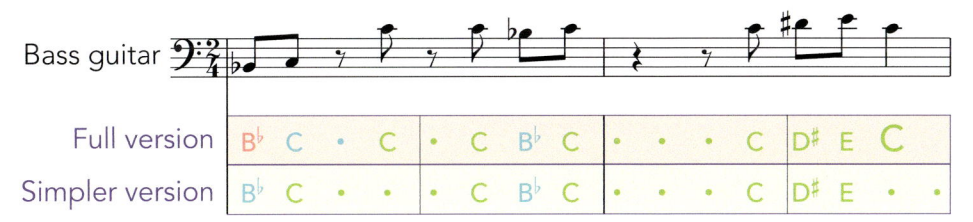

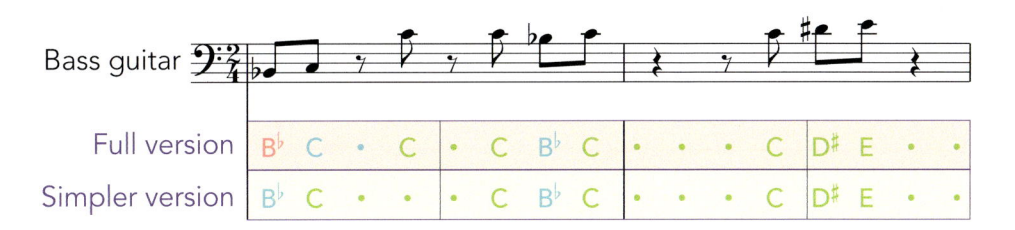

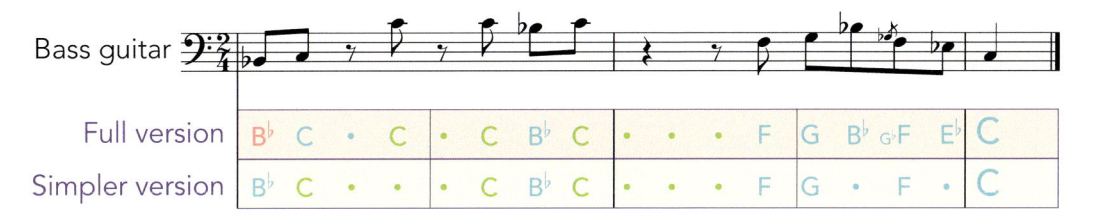

guitar · keys

Bass guitar

| Full version | B♭ | C | · | C | · | C | B♭ | C | · | · | · | C | D♯ | E | · | · |
| Simpler version | B♭ | C | · | · | · | C | B♭ | C | · | · | · | C | D♯ | E | · | · |

Bass / Left hand

Bass guitar

| Full version | B♭ | C | · | C | · | C | B♭ | C | · | · | · | C | D♯ | E | C |
| Simpler version | B♭ | C | · | · | · | C | B♭ | C | · | · | · | C | D♯ | E | · | · |

Bass guitar

| Full version | B♭ | C | · | C | · | C | B♭ | C | · | · | · | C | D♯ | E | · | · |
| Simpler version | B♭ | C | · | · | · | C | B♭ | C | · | · | · | C | D♯ | E | · | · |

Bass guitar

| Full version | B♭ | C | · | C | · | C | B♭ | C | · | · | · | F | G | B♭ | G♭ F | E♭ | C |
| Simpler version | B♭ | C | · | · | · | C | B♭ | C | · | · | · | F | G | · | F | · | C |

Try singing some or all of the rap.

mic

Names of notes on a keyboard

Copyright material from Ockelford, Gray, Cohen and Mai (2023), *Count Me In!*, Routledge

Music-Makers

Before a performance of *Urban Rap*, show participants how to create a short soundscape of digitally recorded short bursts of speech using an app such as GarageBand. Replay the speech montage following Verse 6. For example:

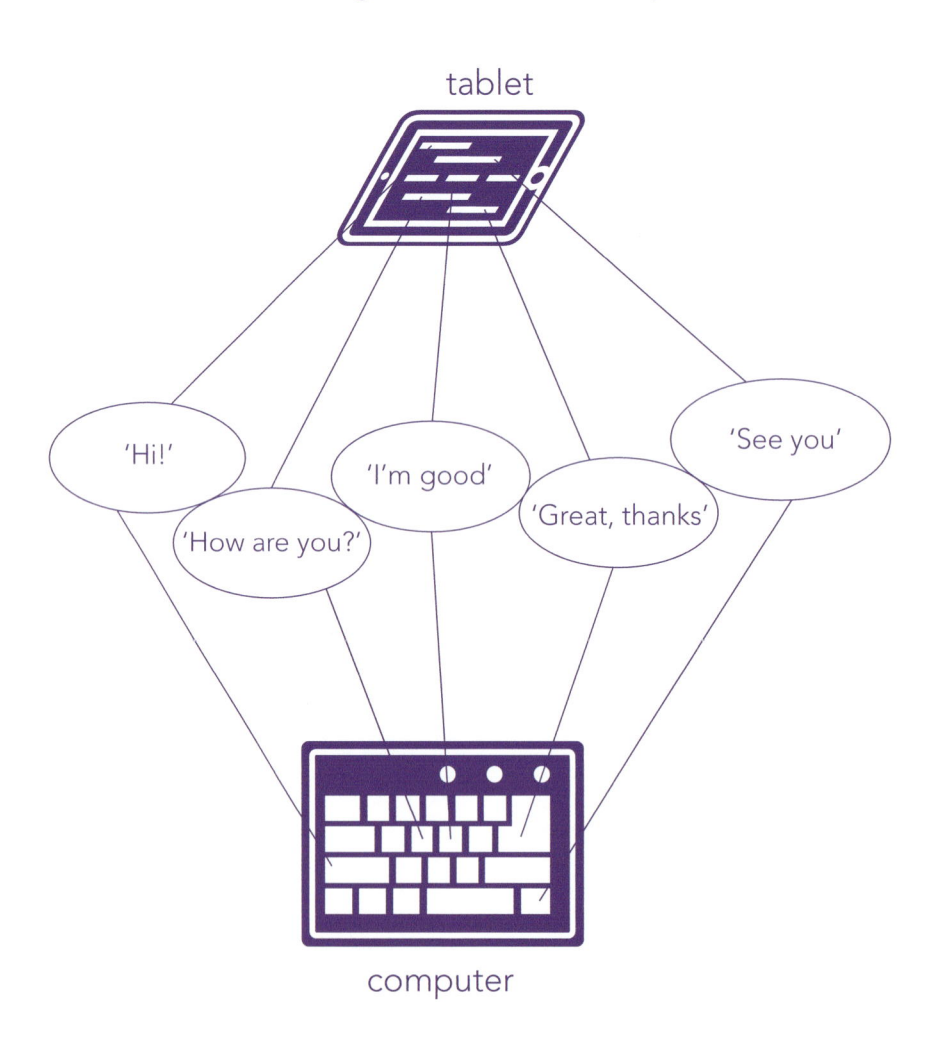

tablet

'Hi!'   'I'm good'   'See you'
'How are you?'   'Great, thanks'

computer

Score for music teachers to use

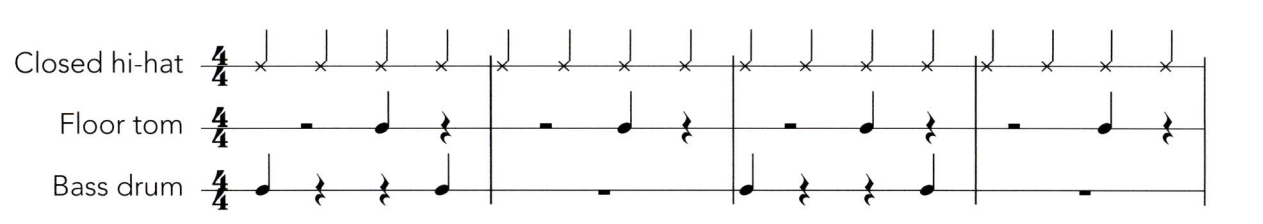

Introduction

Farm Reggae offers an alternative to the children's song *Old MacDonald Had a Farm* which may be more appropriate for young people with disabilities beyond the early years, as it makes use of a contemporary popular style – 'reggae' – that is free from the connotations of early childhood. Reggae originated in Jamaica in the late 1960s and is characterised by an offbeat rhythm section. Its most famous exponent was Bob Marley with his band The Wailers, which had hits such as *Three Little Birds*.

Farm Reggae has a simple structure in which the first five lines are invariably the same, with only the sixth differing each time, as a different animal is identified by its sound. Its very simplicity means that *Farm Reggae* is easy to adapt for different circumstances – a visit to a zoo, for example.

Musical resources required

Choose from the following, according to participants' abilities, preferences and needs:

Sound-Makers

- Wrist bells
- Control of digitally recorded animal sounds through
    - gesture recognition technology (tablets/beams)
    - eye gaze technology
    - switch(es)

  that are loaded with sound files from https://www.soundsofintent.app/count-me-in or elsewhere
- Microphone(s) and amplifier(s), potentially with loop pedal(s) and effects

Pattern-Makers

- Bass drum(s), side drum(s)
- Pattern-making through individually recorded animal sounds using a switch or switches that are loaded with sound files from https://www.soundsofintent.app/count-me-in or elsewhere
- Microphone(s) and amplifier(s), potentially with loop pedal(s) and effects

Motif-Makers

- Wood block(s)
- Keyboard(s), recorder(s) and/or other wind instrument(s)
- Control of digitally recorded animal sounds on
    - tablet(s)
    - computer(s)

  that are loaded with sound files from https://www.soundsofintent.app/count-me-in or elsewhere
- Microphone(s) and amplifier(s), potentially with loop pedal(s) and effects

Music-Makers

- Keyboard(s), recorder(s) and/or other wind instrument(s), tablet(s)
- Guitar(s), ukulele(s), bass guitar(s)
- Control of digitally recorded animal sounds on
    - tablet(s)
    - computer(s)

    that are loaded with sound files from https://www.soundsofintent.app/count-me-in or elsewhere
- Microphone(s) and amplifier(s), potentially with loop pedal(s) and effects

Additional items

Farm Reggae can be performed in a multisensory way, with pictures and/or videos of animals, and perhaps following a visit to a farm. Participants could wear different animal costumes or masks as part of a performance.

Strategies

Introduce *Farm Reggae* to participants by playing a recording (which can be downloaded from https://www.soundsofintent.app/count-me-in) over a few days before working on active engagement. Just listening will help participants to become familiar with the sounds, patterns, motifs, melodies and harmonies that are used. This follows the model that occurs naturally in musical development – and in aural traditions – of listening preceding active participation.

Practise individual parts one-to-one, and then in pairs or small groups, before bringing the whole texture together.

Using the backing track, start each verse with sound-makers, then pattern-makers and motif-makers before song-makers come in with the main melody. The arrangements will suit participants at all levels of musical development. If some choose not to play or sing, the backing track will hold things together.

Links to other areas of experience and learning

In schools and colleges, *Farm Reggae* has potential links to other curricular areas, such as geography (agriculture), and contemporary history (awareness of Jamaican society and its cultural diaspora).

Farm

Sound-Makers

During each verse

Encourage participants to shake the wrist bells or ankle bells from time to time.

wrist bells

Or help them make similar sounds by activating digitally recorded jingly bell sounds using gesture recognition technology such as that available on tablets and using beams,

beam

tablet

or by using switches or eye gaze technology.

switch

eye gaze

Verses 1, 2, 3, 4, 5, 6, 7

Down on the farm,
Just you and me.
What can you hear?
What can it be?
Listen carefully.

Copyright material from Ockelford, Gray, Cohen and Mai (2023), *Count Me In!*, Routledge

Reggae

Sound-Makers

After verses

Encourage participants to trigger appropriate pre-recorded animal sounds using switches, or gesture recognition technology using tablets or beams.

switch

tablet

beam

It's a cow.

It's a hen.

It's a horse.

It's a sheep.

It's a dog.

It's a pig.

It's a cat.

Some participants may be able to vocalise sounds that resemble the sounds of some animals; their efforts can be amplified or enhanced using a microphone and amplifier.

mic

Copyright material from Ockelford, Gray, Cohen and Mai (2023), *Count Me In!*, Routledge

Pattern-Makers

During each verse

Model for participants how to join with in the regular beats in the song on different percussion instruments, such as a large (bass) drum and smaller (side) drum. Reggae has a strong 'back beat'. To fit this in with the music, it may be easiest at first to play the drums alternately, left hand, right hand, and so on.

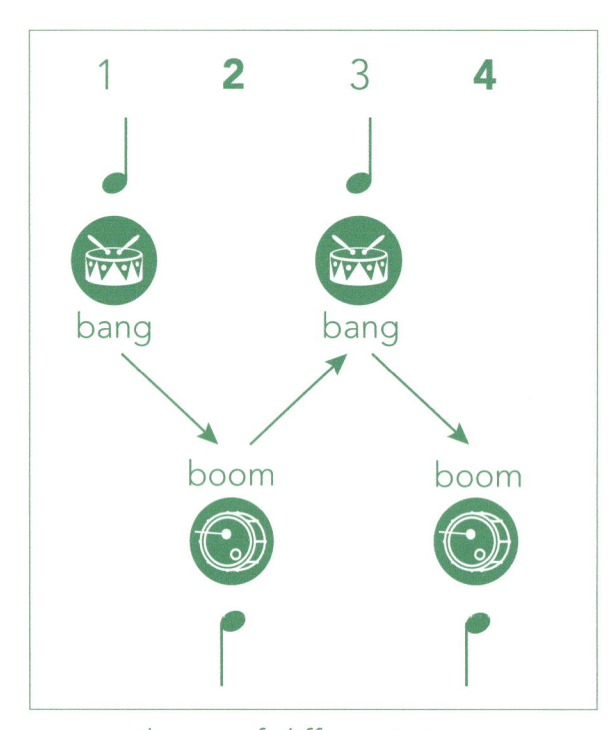

1	**2**	3	**4**
bang	bang		
	boom		boom

drums of different sizes

The try the large drum alone.

1	**2**	3	**4**
	boom		boom

large drum

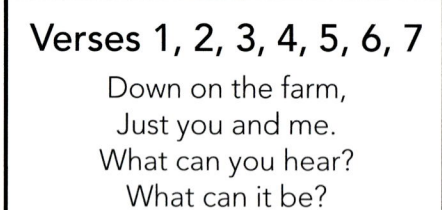

Verses 1, 2, 3, 4, 5, 6, 7

Down on the farm,
Just you and me.
What can you hear?
What can it be?
Listen carefully.

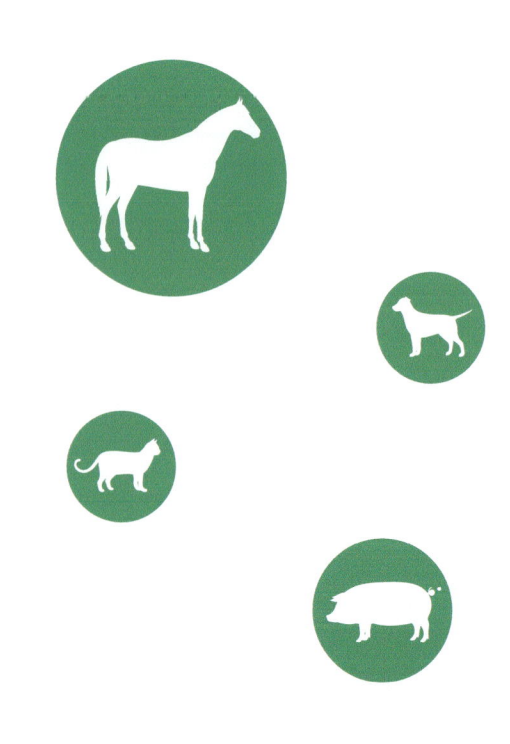

Pattern-Makers

After verses

Show participants how to trigger appropriate pre-recorded animal sounds using switches or the touchscreens on tablets, and make patterns with them by repeating the sounds. For example:

'oink' 'oink' 'oink'

switch

'woof' 'woof' 'woof'

tablet

Some participants may be able to make vocal patterns that resemble repeated animal sounds; their efforts can be amplified or enhanced using a microphone and amplifier.

mic

It's a cow.
It's a hen.
It's a horse.
It's a sheep.
It's a dog.
It's a pig.
It's a cat.

Copyright material from Ockelford, Gray, Cohen and Mai (2023), *Count Me In!*, Routledge

Motif-Makers

During each verse

Help participants to join in with the groove of the piece with short bursts of rhythm on a wood block. To keep the rhythm on track, try thinking of words that fit. For example:

'down   on   the   farm'

wood block

Try picking out a short fragment of melody from the accompaniment and encourage participants to join in where appropriate by singing or playing. Again, it may help to think of a word or words to keep things on track.

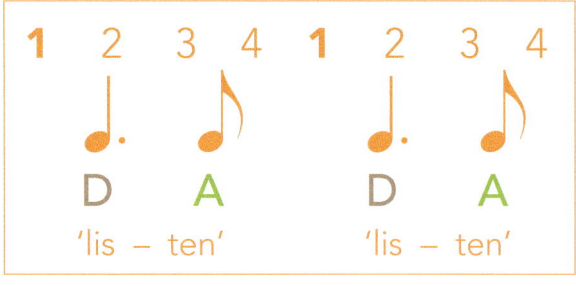

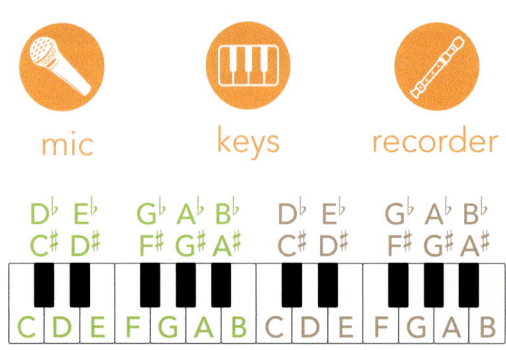

1 2 3 4 **1** 2 3 4
D A D A
'lis – ten'   'lis – ten'

mic   keys   recorder

Names of notes on a keyboard

Verses 1, 2, 3, 4, 5, 6, 7

Down on the farm,
Just you and me.
What can you hear?
What can it be?
Listen carefully.

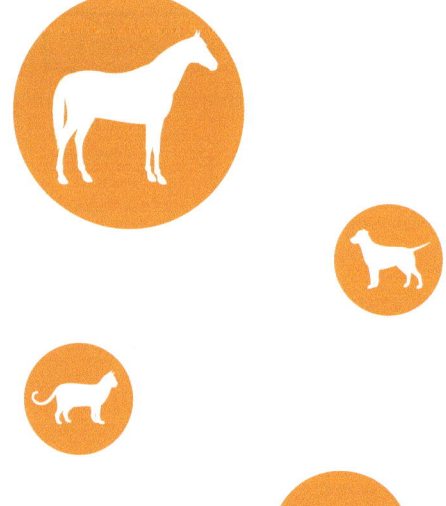

Copyright material from Ockelford, Gray, Cohen and Mai (2023), *Count Me In!*, Routledge

Reggae

Motif-Makers

After verses

Demonstrate 'call and response' activities using short improvised groups of animal sounds, choosing from digital collections of sounds triggered by keys on computers or the screens of tablets or phones. For example:

It's a cow.
It's a hen.
It's a horse.
It's a sheep.
It's a dog.
It's a pig.
It's a cat.

CALL

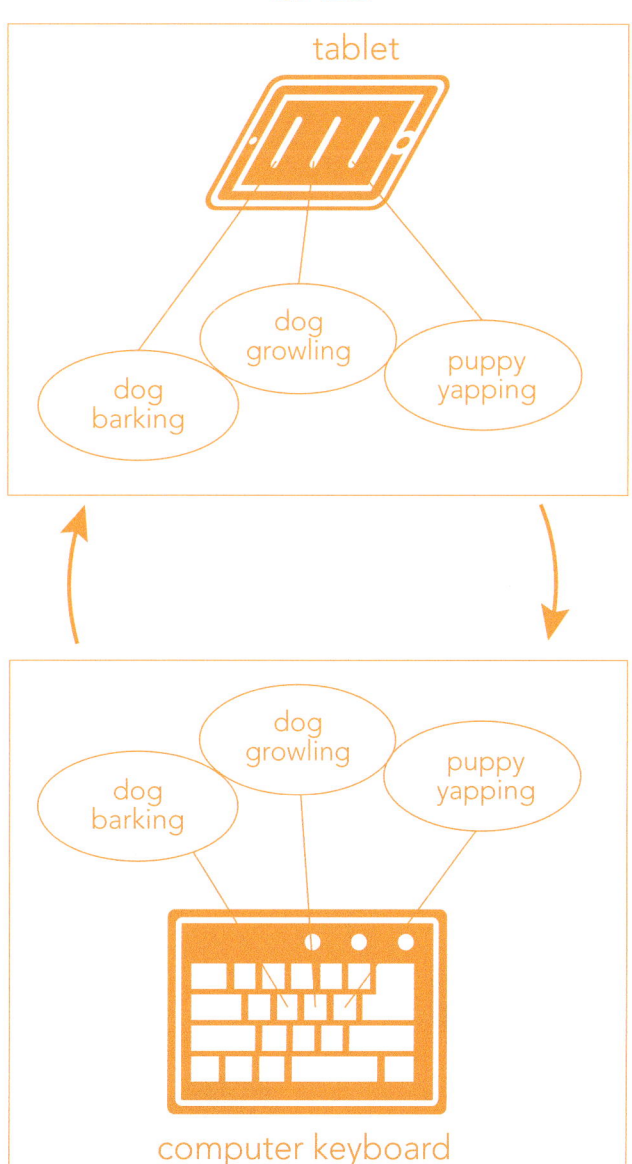

tablet — dog barking, dog growling, puppy yapping

RESPONSE

computer keyboard — dog barking, dog growling, puppy yapping

Copyright material from Ockelford, Gray, Cohen and Mai (2023), *Count Me In!*, Routledge

Farm

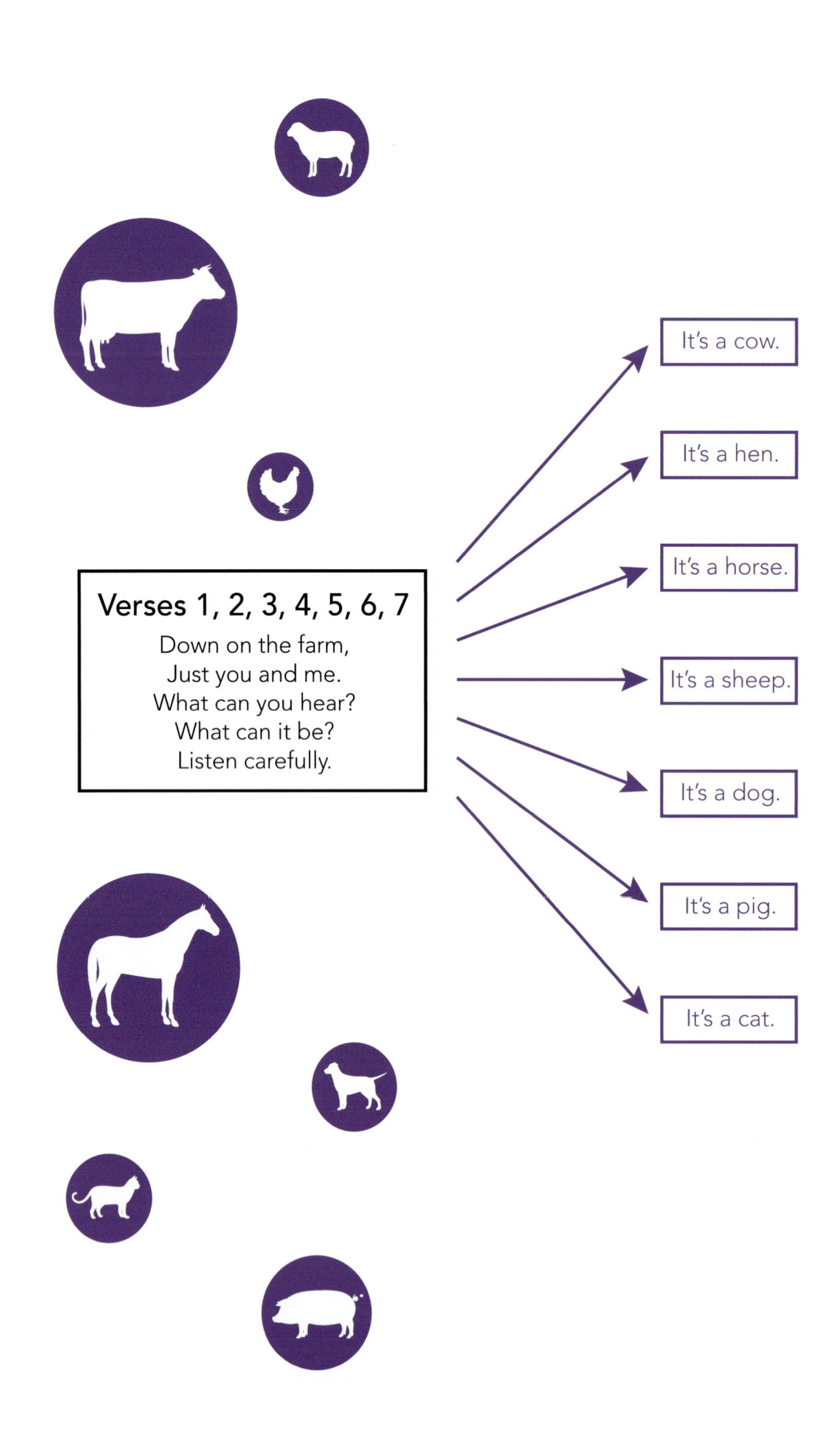

Verses 1, 2, 3, 4, 5, 6, 7

Down on the farm,
Just you and me.
What can you hear?
What can it be?
Listen carefully.

- It's a cow.
- It's a hen.
- It's a horse.
- It's a sheep.
- It's a dog.
- It's a pig.
- It's a cat.

Reggae

Music-Makers
During each verse

Teach participants to sing or play the tune on a melody instrument (such as a keyboard or recorder), and/or to play the bass line on a keyboard or bass guitar. Show them how to play the chords on a keyboard, guitar or ukulele, using simpler versions if preferred.

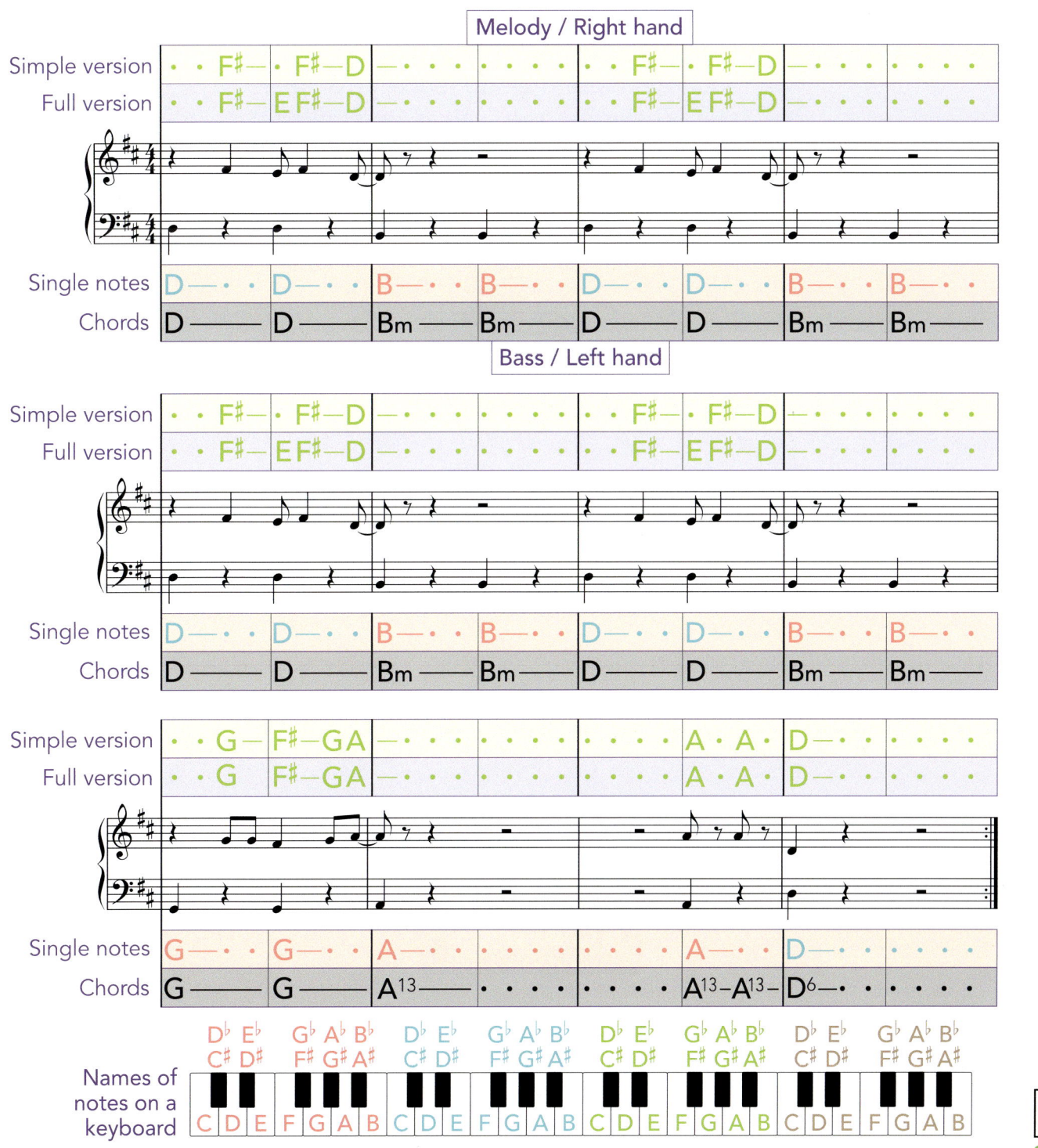

keys · recorder · bass · guitar · ukulele

Melody / Right hand

Simple version	· · F#— · F#—D	— · · ·	· · · ·	· · · ·	· · F#— · F#—D	— · · ·	· · · ·
Full version	· · F#—E F#—D	— · · ·	· · · ·	· · · ·	· · F#—E F#—D	— · · ·	· · · ·

Single notes	D— · ·	D— · ·	B— · ·	B— · ·	D— · ·	D— · ·	B— · ·	B— · ·
Chords	D	D	Bm	Bm	D	D	Bm	Bm

Bass / Left hand

Simple version	· · F#— · F#—D	— · · ·	· · · ·	· · · ·	· · F#— · F#—D	— · · ·	· · · ·
Full version	· · F#—E F#—D	— · · ·	· · · ·	· · · ·	· · F#—E F#—D	— · · ·	· · · ·

Single notes	D— · ·	D— · ·	B— · ·	B— · ·	D— · ·	D— · ·	B— · ·	B— · ·
Chords	D	D	Bm	Bm	D	D	Bm	Bm

Simple version	· · G— F#—GA	— · · ·	· · · ·	· · · ·	· · A · A · D—	· · · ·
Full version	· · G F#—GA	— · · ·	· · · ·	· · · ·	· · A · A · D—	· · · ·

Single notes	G— · ·	G— · ·	A— · ·	· · · ·	· · · ·	A— · ·	D— · · ·
Chords	G———	G	A¹³———	· · · ·	· · · ·	A¹³—A¹³—	D⁶—— · · · ·

Names of notes on a keyboard

Music-Makers

After verses

Before a performance of *Farm Reggae*, assist participants in creating a short soundscape of digitally recorded animal sounds using an app such as GarageBand. Replay the montage of animal sounds at the appropriate points following one verse or more. For example:

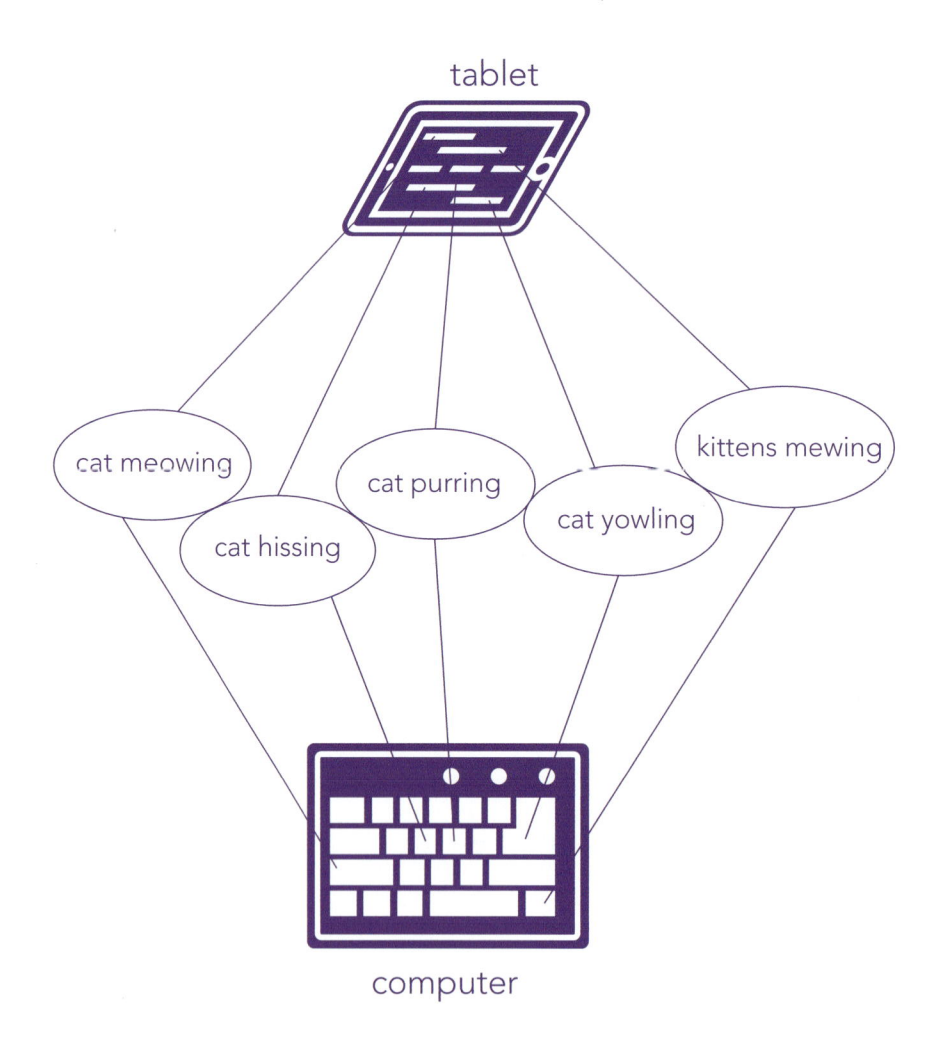

tablet

- cat meowing
- cat hissing
- cat purring
- cat yowling
- kittens mewing

computer

Reggae

Score for music teachers to use

(Verse lyrics:)

Down on the farm,

Just you and me. What can you hear?

What can it be? Lis-ten care-ful-ly

It's a cow.
hen.
horse.
sheep.
dog.
pig.
cat.

Bollywood

Introduction

Bollywood is the world's largest film industry. Its name comes from a fusion of 'Hollywood' and 'Bombay' (the old name for the city in India that is now called 'Mumbai'). Among the highlights of Bollywood films are elaborate dance sequences set to music, which combine features of India's classical and folk traditions with Western pop, jazz and hip-hop. The core of *Bollywood Party Dance* is a chorus in 'ABA' form: that is, an opening section and a middle section that is followed by a reprise of the opening. It is written for alternating voices, with some overlap at the ends of lines. The themes are food, drink and having fun! There are rapid streams of words set over a repeating two-bar phrase, which provides a pulsating harmonic and rhythmic backdrop to the song.

The chorus is heard five times. Each has parts for sound-makers, pattern-makers, motif-makers and music-makers. This means that everyone, no matter what their level of musical development, can join in. Between appearances of the chorus there are improvised sections, using party sounds that can be downloaded from the *Count Me In!* pages on the Sounds of Intent website. Each is intended for players and singers who are able to engage with music in different ways. The first is for sound-makers, the second for pattern-makers, the third for motif-makers, and the fourth for music-makers.

Musical resources required

Choose from the following, according to participants' abilities, preferences and needs:

Sound-Makers

- Finger cymbal(s)
- Control of digitally recorded finger cymbal sounds and party sounds through
    - gesture recognition technology (tablets/beams)
    - eye gaze technology
    - switch(es)

  that are loaded with sound files from https://www.soundsofintent.app/count-me-in
- Microphone(s) and amplifier(s), potentially with loop pedal(s) and effects

Pattern-Makers

- Drum(s), wood block(s)
- Pattern-making through individually recorded percussive sounds or short party sounds such as party poppers, using a switch or switches, or tablet(s) that are loaded with sound files from https://www.soundsofintent.app/count-me-in

Party Dance

Motif-Makers

- Cabasa(s), cowbell(s)
- Tablet(s) or computer keyboard(s) loaded with short party sounds from https://www.soundsofintent.app/count-me-in

Music-Makers

- Keyboard(s), recorder(s), other wind instrument(s), tablet(s)
- Guitar(s), ukulele(s), bass guitar(s)
- Tablet(s) or computer keyboard(s) loaded with short party sounds from https://www.soundsofintent.app/count-me-in

Additional items

As its name suggests, *Bollywood Party Dance* can be performed in a multisensory way, including movement and dance, and using props such as streamers, sashes, ribbons, coloured lights, party poppers and sparklers. Participants could dress up for a party, and the performance could be followed by the consumption of food and drink!

Strategies

The best way to approach *Bollywood Party Dance* is to encourage participants to listen to it a number of times over a few days before asking them to join in. This will enable them to become familiar with the sounds, patterns, motifs, melodies and harmonies that are used.

Individual parts can be practised one-to-one, and then in pairs or small groups, before attempting to bring the whole song together.

To join in with the verses, play the backing track and start with sound-makers, then pattern-makers and motif-makers, before song-makers come in with the main melody. The arrangements are designed to accommodate the needs and abilities of participants at all levels of musical development. If some are not present or choose not to play or sing, the backing track will hold things together.

Links to other areas of experience and learning

In schools and colleges, *Bollywood Party Dance* has potential links to other curricular areas, such as geography (South Asian culture and the Indian diaspora).

Bollywood

Sound-Makers

During each verse

Help participants to ding the finger cymbals from time to time; they may be easiest to use if they are suspended from a stand.

finger cymbals

Or help them make similar sounds by activating digitally recorded finger cymbal sounds using gesture recognition technology such as that available on tablets and using beams,

beam

tablet

or by using switches or eye gaze technology.

switch

eye gaze

Verses 1, 2, 3, 4, 5

Lots of food to eat,
We'll all have a treat.
It's party, party, party time.
Bottles are on show,
Drink is sure to flow.
It's party, party, party time.

Nuts and cuts of meat in strips,
Chips and dips and parsley tips.
Sticky rice and choc'late mice,
Quiche and hummus, pretzel bites.
Pies and fries and sausage rolls.
Avocado mash in bowls.
Sweets and treats and party mix,
Fritters, brownies, cheese on sticks.

Party Dance

Sound-Makers

After Verse 1

Show participants how to trigger pre-recorded party sounds, such as sparklers and the hubbub of people laughing and chatting, using a switch or switches, tablet(s), beam(s) or eye gaze technology.

- switch
- tablet
- beam
- eye gaze

Participants may be able to vocalise party sounds, which can be amplified and enhanced using effects such as reverberation, and repeated using a loop pedal.

- mic

- **One-off party sounds**
- Patterns of party sounds
- Call and response groups of party sounds
- Montage of party sounds

Copyright material from Ockelford, Gray, Cohen and Mai (2023), *Count Me In!*, Routledge

Bollywood

Pattern-Makers

During each verse

Encourage participants to join in the regular beat of the song on the drum, wood block or tambourine, for example, or by using a switch or tablet onto which single sounds like these have been downloaded. The beat could be slow (in time with *party, party, party*) or quicker (in time with *nuts* and *cuts* of *meat* in *strips*).

Verses 1, 2, 3, 4, 5

Lots of food to eat,
We'll all have a treat.
It's party, party, party time.
Bottles are on show,
Drink is sure to flow.
It's party, party, party time.

Nuts and cuts of meat in strips,
Chips and dips and parsley tips.
Sticky rice and choc'late mice,
Quiche and hummus, pretzel bites.
Pies and fries and sausage rolls.
Avocado mash in bowls.
Sweets and treats and party mix,
Fritters, brownies, cheese on sticks.

'*party,*   *party*   *party*'

bang   bang   bang

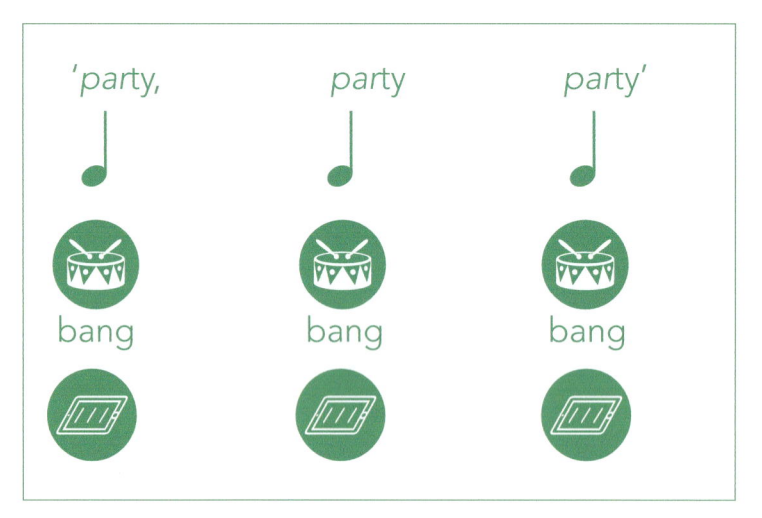

drum (or drum sound on tablet)
(slower beat)

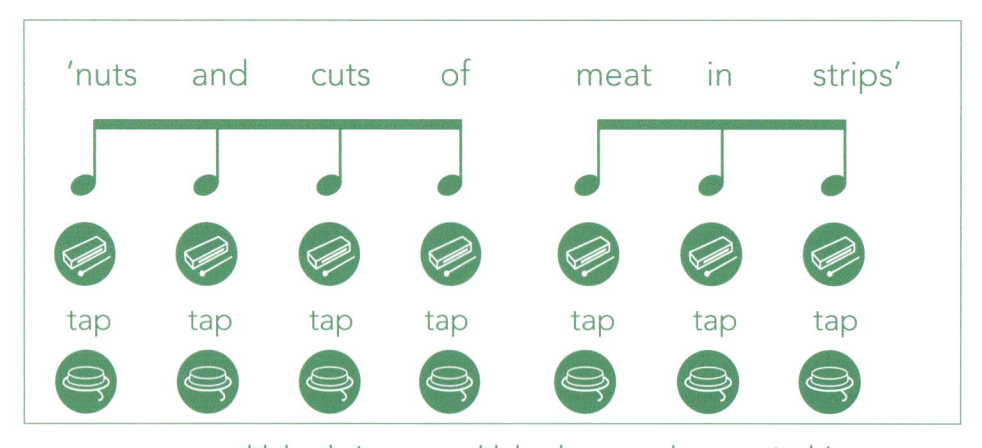

'nuts   and   cuts   of   meat   in   strips'

tap   tap   tap   tap   tap   tap   tap

wood block (or wood block sound on switch)
(quicker beat)

Copyright material from Ockelford, Gray, Cohen and Mai (2023), *Count Me In!*, Routledge

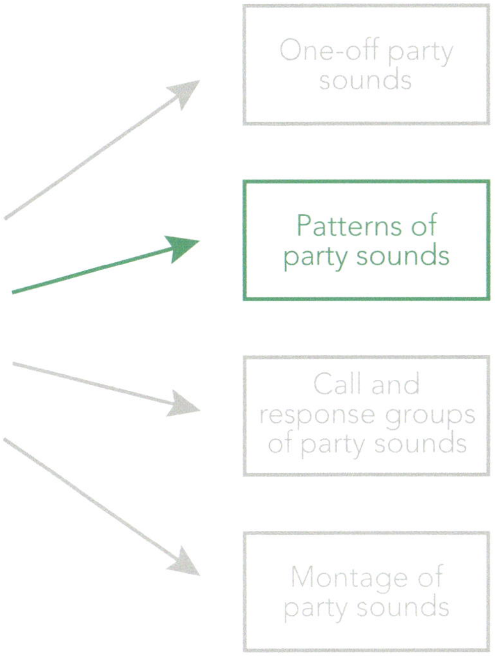

Party Dance

Pattern-Makers

After Verse 2

Show participants how to trigger short pre-recorded party sounds, such as party poppers, the clink of glasses or someone saying 'cheers' using a switch or switches or tablet, and repeat them to make simple patterns.

- One-off party sounds
- **Patterns of party sounds**
- Call and response groups of party sounds
- Montage of party sounds

switch (linked to party popper sound)

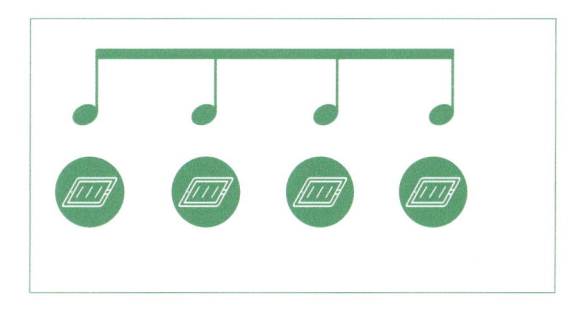

tablet (linked to sound of clinking glasses or someone saying 'cheers')

Copyright material from Ockelford, Gray, Cohen and Mai (2023), *Count Me In!*, Routledge

Bollywood

Motif-Makers

During each verse

Encourage participants to join in with the main rhythms of the song on a cowbell or cabasa. Think of the words (or sing them) to keep the rhythms on track.

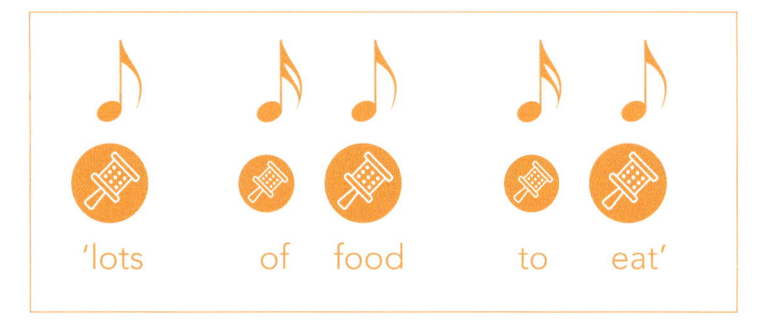

'lots   of   food   to   eat'

wood block

'par_____ty,   par_____ty'

cowbell

Verses 1, 2, 3, 4, 5

Lots of food to eat,
We'll all have a treat.
It's party, party, party time.
Bottles are on show,
Drink is sure to flow.
It's party, party, party time.

Nuts and cuts of meat in strips,
Chips and dips and parsley tips.
Sticky rice and choc'late mice,
Quiche and hummus, pretzel bites.
Pies and fries and sausage rolls.
Avocado mash in bowls.
Sweets and treats and party mix,
Fritters, brownies, cheese on sticks.

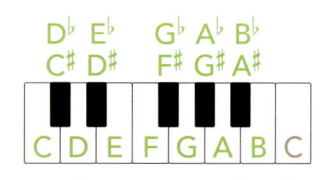

Some participants may be able to play the motifs on a melody instrument.

E   E   E   F#   G

D E D   D E D

'par_____ty,   par_____ty'

Names of notes on a keyboard

Party Dance

Motif-Makers

After Verse 3

Demonstrate how it is possible to connect different groups of party sounds – such as party poppers, clinking of glasses and people saying 'cheers' – together in different ways, choosing from digital collections of sounds triggered by keys on computers or the touch screens of tablets or phones

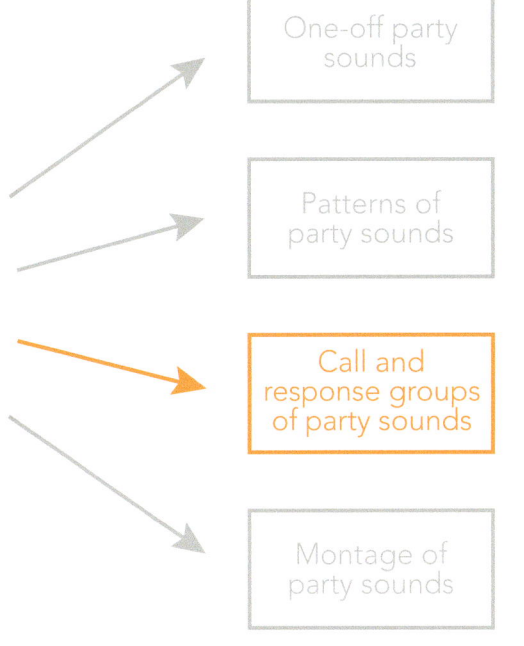

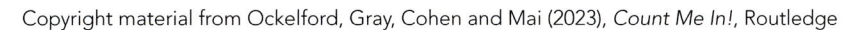

- One-off party sounds
- Patterns of party sounds
- **Call and response groups of party sounds**
- Montage of party sounds

tablet

party poppers · clink of glasses · 'cheers'

computer keyboard

Copyright material from Ockelford, Gray, Cohen and Mai (2023), *Count Me In!*, Routledge

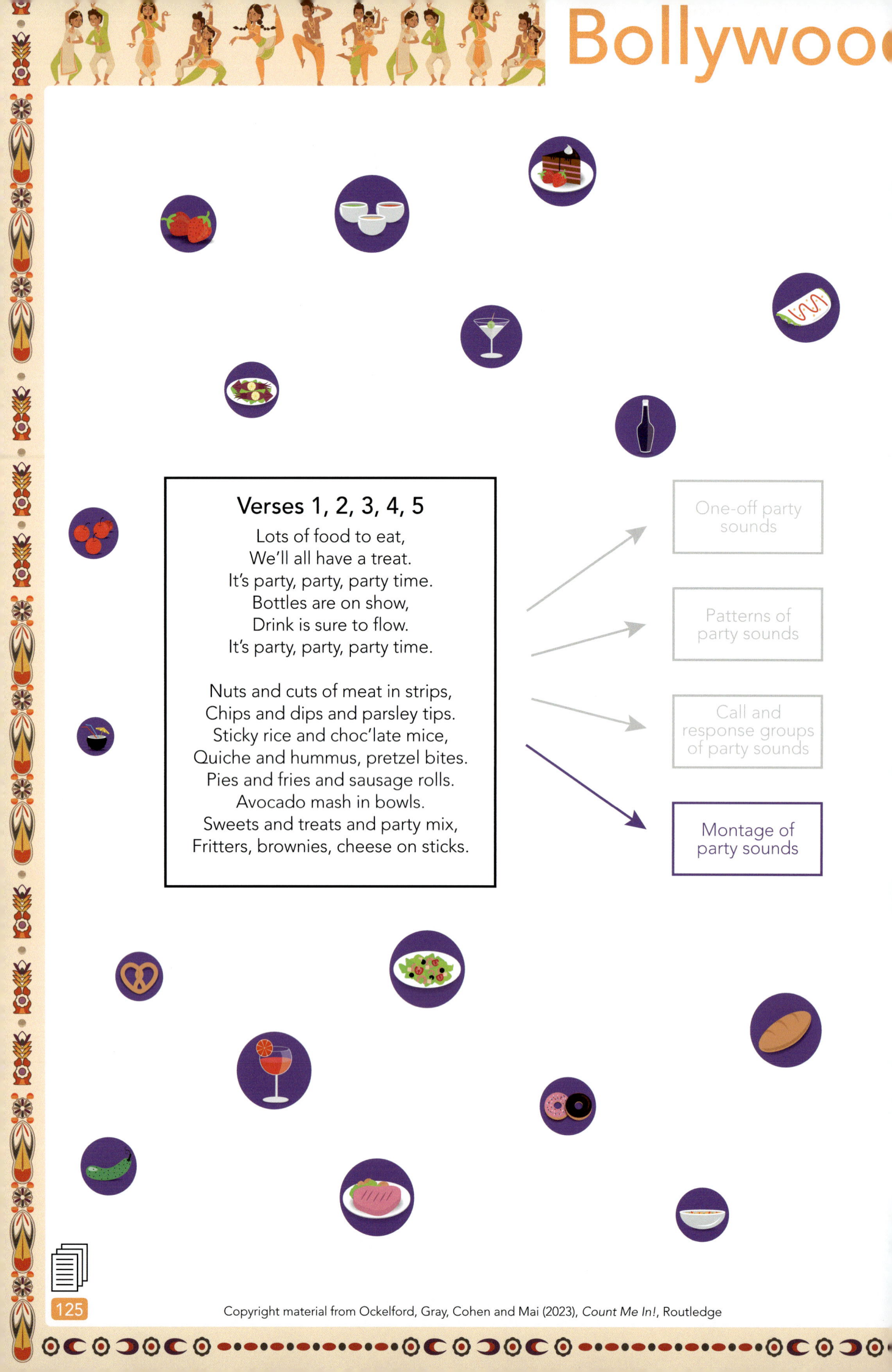

Bollywood

Verses 1, 2, 3, 4, 5

Lots of food to eat,
We'll all have a treat.
It's party, party, party time.
Bottles are on show,
Drink is sure to flow.
It's party, party, party time.

Nuts and cuts of meat in strips,
Chips and dips and parsley tips.
Sticky rice and choc'late mice,
Quiche and hummus, pretzel bites.
Pies and fries and sausage rolls.
Avocado mash in bowls.
Sweets and treats and party mix,
Fritters, brownies, cheese on sticks.

- One-off party sounds
- Patterns of party sounds
- Call and response groups of party sounds
- **Montage of party sounds**

Copyright material from Ockelford, Gray, Cohen and Mai (2023), *Count Me In!*, Routledge

Party Dance

Music-Makers

After Verse 4

Before a performance of *Bollywood Party Dance* help participants to create a short soundscape of digitally recorded party sounds using an app such as GarageBand. Replay the montage of party sounds after Verse 4.

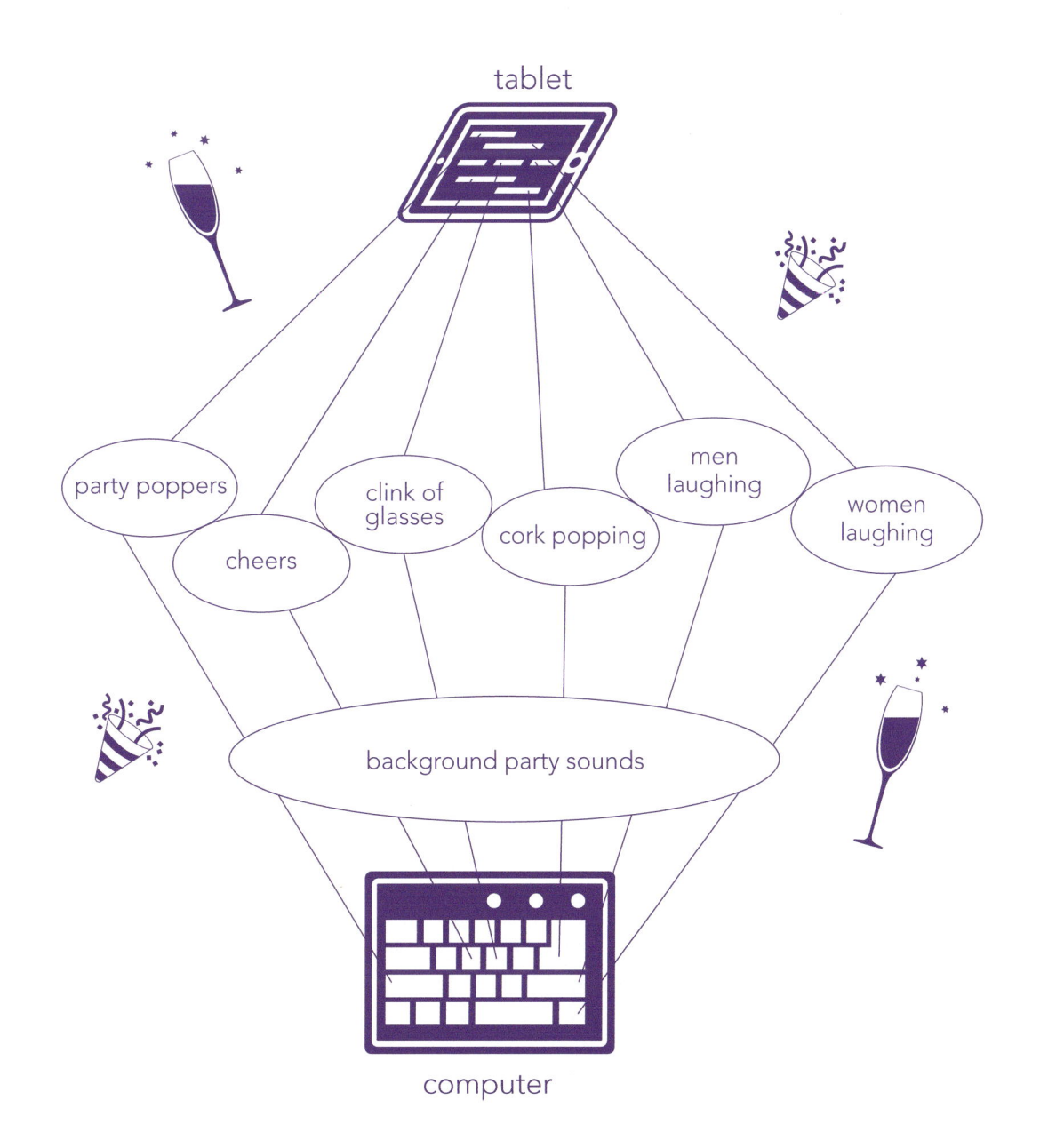

tablet

- party poppers
- cheers
- clink of glasses
- cork popping
- men laughing
- women laughing

background party sounds

computer

Bollywood

Music-Makers
During each verse

Teach participants to sing or play the two parts of the tune on melody instruments (such as keyboards or recorders), and/or play the bass line on a keyboard or bass guitar. Model how to play the chords on a keyboard, guitar or ukulele.

- keys
- recorder
- bass
- guitar
- ukulele

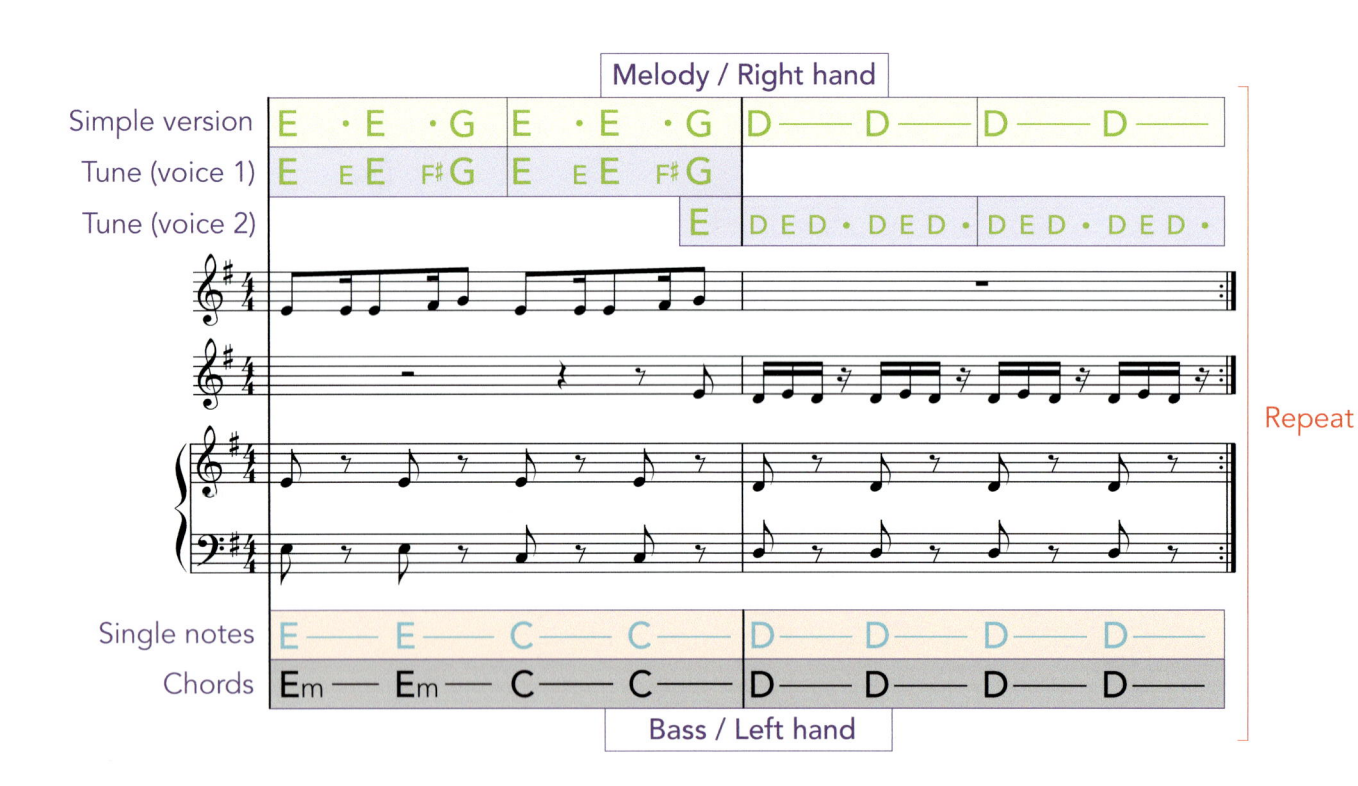

Melody / Right hand

Simple version	E · E · G	E · E · G	D — D	D — D
Tune (voice 1)	E ᴇ E F♯G	E ᴇ E F♯G		
Tune (voice 2)			E D E D · D E D ·	D E D · D E D ·

Repeat

Bass / Left hand

Single notes	E — E —	C — C —	D — D —	D — D —
Chords	Em — Em —	C — C —	D — D —	D — D —

Names of notes on a keyboard: 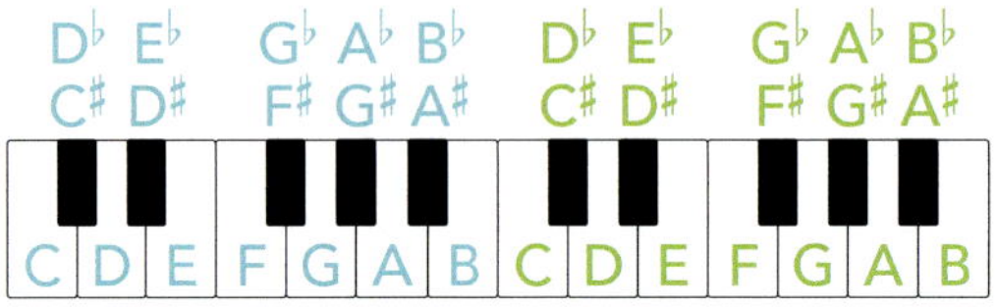
D♭ E♭ / C♯ D♯ — C D E
G♭ A♭ B♭ / F♯ G♯ A♯ — F G A B
D♭ E♭ / C♯ D♯ — C D E
G♭ A♭ B♭ / F♯ G♯ A♯ — F G A B

Party Dance

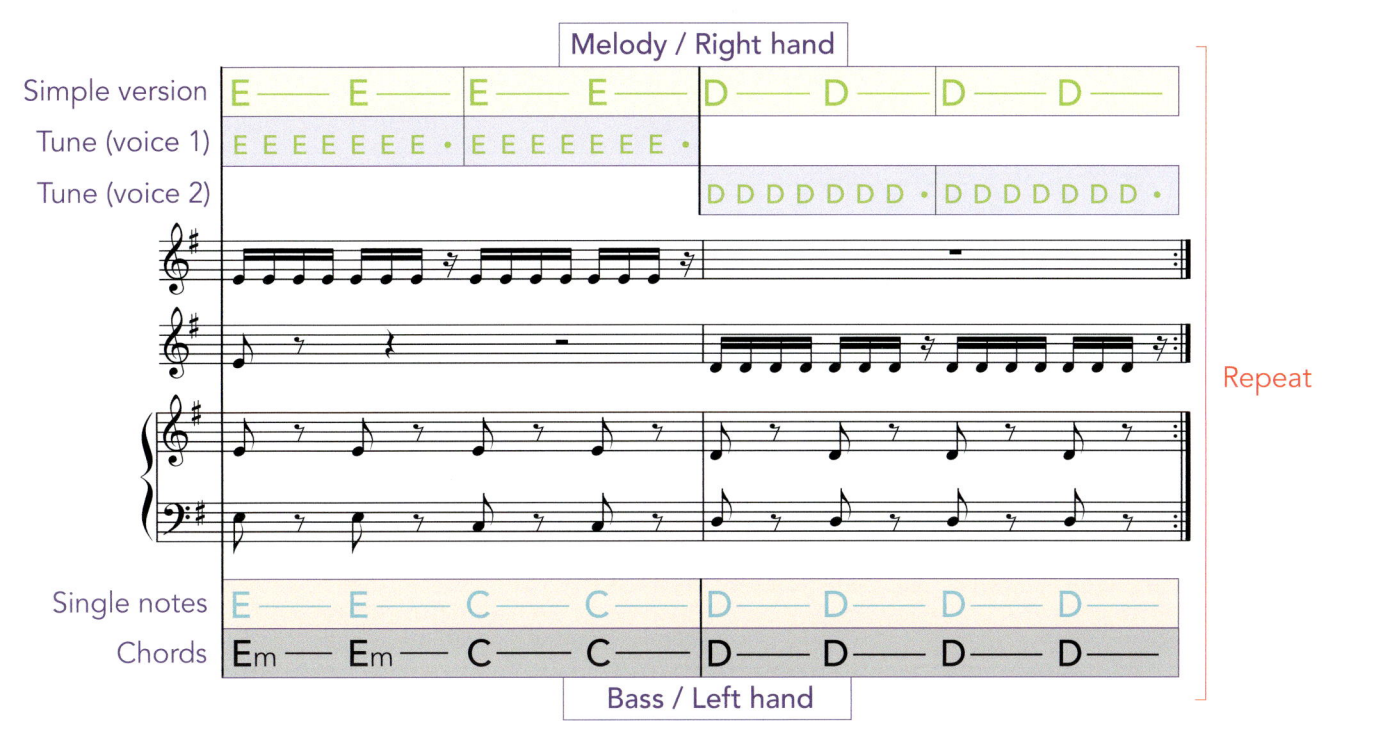

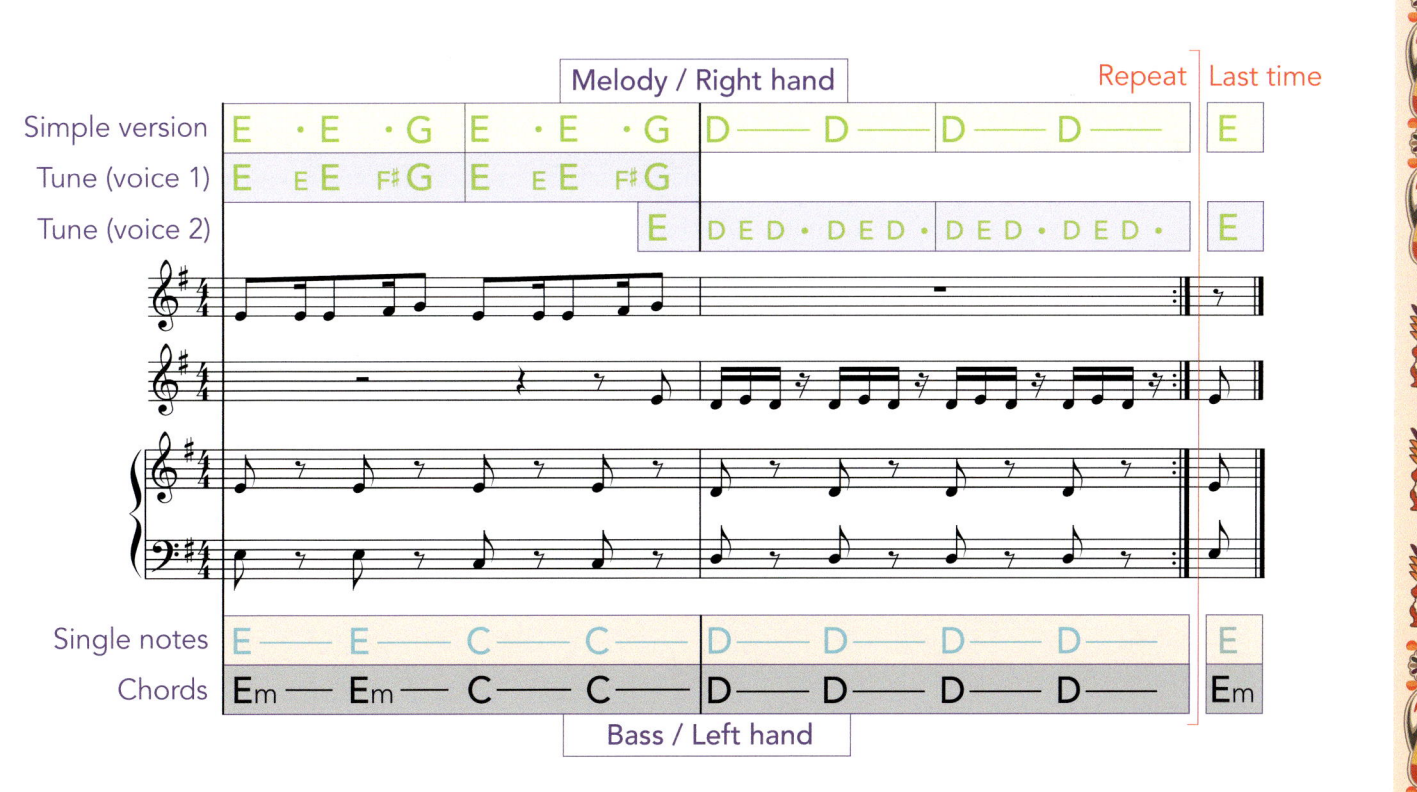

Bollywood

Score for music teachers to use

Keyboard — Em / C / D / Repeat as required

Voice:

Lots of food to eat, We'll all have a treat. It's par—ty, par—ty, par—ty, par—ty,

time. It's par—ty, par—ty, par—ty, par—ty,

Bot-tles are on show, Drink is sure to flow.

time.

Nuts and cuts of meat in strips, Chips and dips and pars-ley tips.

Sti-cky rice and choc'late mice, Quiche and hum-mus, pret-zel bites.

Pies and fries and sau-sage rolls, A - vo - ca - do mash in bowls.

Sweets and treats and par-ty mix, Frit-ters, brown-ies, cheese on sticks.

It's par—ty, par—ty, par—ty, par—ty,

Lots of food to eat, We'll all have a treat.

time. It's par—ty, par—ty, par—ty, par—ty time.

Bot-tles are on show, Drink is sure to flow.

Copyright material from Ockelford, Gray, Cohen and Mai (2023), *Count Me In!*, Routledge

Party Dance

Sound-makers get to grips with participation in the *Bollywood Party Dance*

Introduction

Spy Soundtrack draws its inspiration from the music and sound effects used in the James Bond films. The bass line comprises an 'ostinato' (a short repeated phrase) with a driving, syncopated rhythm on a single note: E. The musical tension rises and falls as phrases of the melody and their accompanying chords move away from the bass, sounding gradually more discordant, and then change, sometimes suddenly, to fit in with it again. There are two main themes, the first played on the trumpet and the second on a group of brass instruments, sounding in close harmony. The themes are jazzy and peppered with blues notes. There are no lyrics, but the structure of the music is articulated by the solos and brass ensemble sections: 'Introduction', 'Trumpet solo 1', 'Brass section 1', 'Trumpet solo 2', 'Brass section 2' and 'Trumpet solo 3'.

Spy Soundtrack has two of these instrumental 'verses', with parts that are suitable for sound-makers, pattern-makers, motif-makers and music-makers to join in. The verses are intended to be separated by an improvised section, in which participants can contribute sounds, patterns, motifs, melodies, harmonies and rhythms from those suggested, or they could add their own ideas to the dramatic soundscape.

Musical resources required

Choose from the following according to participants' abilities, preferences and needs:

Sound-Makers

- Chime bar(s), tubular bell(s), playing the note E
- Control of digitally recorded Es through
    - gesture recognition technology (tablets/beams)
    - eye gaze technology
    - switch(es)

    that are loaded with sound files from https://www.soundsofintent.app/count-me-in
- Microphone(s), amplifier(s), loop pedal(s)

Pattern-Makers

- Drum(s) (two different sizes), tubular bells, chime bar(s)
- Pattern-making through individually recorded short spy movie sounds, using a switch or switches that are loaded with sound files from https://www.soundsofintent.app/count-me-in

Soundtrack

Motif-Makers

- Drum(s)
- Keyboard(s), guitar(s), bass guitar(s), ukulele(s)
- Control of digitally recorded spy movie sounds through computers or tablets that are loaded with sound files from https://www.soundsofintent.app/count-me-in

Music-Makers

- Keyboard(s), recorder(s) and/or other wind instrument(s) and/or tablet(s)
- Guitar(s), ukulele(s), bass guitar(s)

Additional items

Spy Soundtrack can be performed as part of a multimedia production involving acting and/or making videos. The sound effects could stimulate ideas for action, or a dramatic scene or interaction could be used to trigger ideas for additional sounds and music.

Strategies

Listen to *Spy Soundtrack* a number of times over the period of a few days before encouraging participants to join in, to enable them to get to know some of the sounds, patterns, motifs, melodies and harmonies that appear in the piece. Participants may naturally start to join in (or indicate that they wish to) when they are ready. It is better to allow more time just for listening rather than putting pressure on people to join in before they are ready.

It may be best to run through individual parts one-to-one before working in pairs or small groups and attempting to bring the whole texture together.

Using the backing track, start with sound-makers, then pattern-makers and motif-makers before music-makers come in with the main melodies. The arrangements are designed to suit all participants, whatever their capacity to engage with sound and music. If some are not present in a particular group, or choose not to play or sing, the backing track will hold things together.

Links to other areas of experience and learning

In schools and colleges, *Spy Soundtrack* can be linked to other curricular areas, in particular drama and media studies.

Sound-Makers

During each verse

Help participants to play a chime bar or tubular bell tuned to E from time to time.

chime bar

tubular bells

Or show them how to activate digitally recorded notes using gesture recognition technology such as that available on tablets and using beams,

tablet

beam

or by using switches or eye gaze technology.

switch

eye gaze

The same note (E) will fit with the music at any time.

Instrumental Section 1

Introduction
Trumpet solo 1
Brass section 1
Trumpet solo 2
Brass section 2
Trumpet solo 3

Instrumental Section 2

Introduction
Trumpet solo 1
Brass section 1
Trumpet solo 2
Brass section 2
Trumpet solo 3

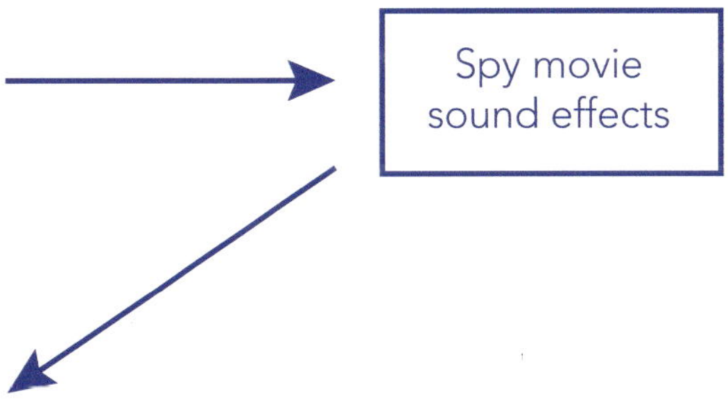

Soundtrack

Sound-Makers

During the sound effects section

Show participants how to trigger pre-recorded spy movie sounds, including cars screeching, a helicopter flying overhead, explosions and the sound of a gadget, using switches, gesture recognition technology on tablets or via a beam, or by utilising eye gaze technology.

Spy movie sound effects

- switch
- eye gaze
- tablet
- beam

The vocal sounds that some participants make naturally may fit well in the mix. They could be enhanced using a microphone, amplifier and, potentially, digital effects including a loop pedal.

- mic

Copyright material from Ockelford, Gray, Cohen and Mai (2023), *Count Me In!*, Routledge

Pattern-Makers

During each verse

Show participants how to join in with the regular beats on unpitched percussion instruments such as the drum or tambourine, or on any tuned percussion instrument, like the glockenspiel or tubular bells, playing the note E. There are slow beats and quicker ones that can be played together. Assistive technology could be used to enable participants with different patterns of movement to achieve the same effects.

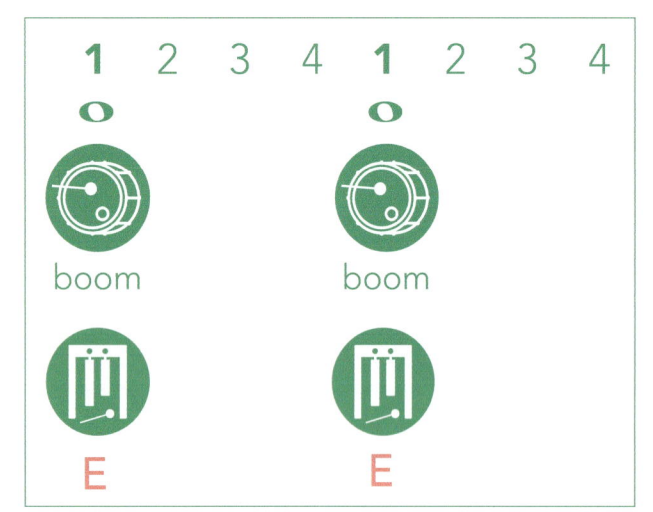

Instrumental Section 1

Introduction
Trumpet solo 1
Brass section 1
Trumpet solo 2
Brass section 2
Trumpet solo 3

bass drum and tubular bells being played with a slow beat

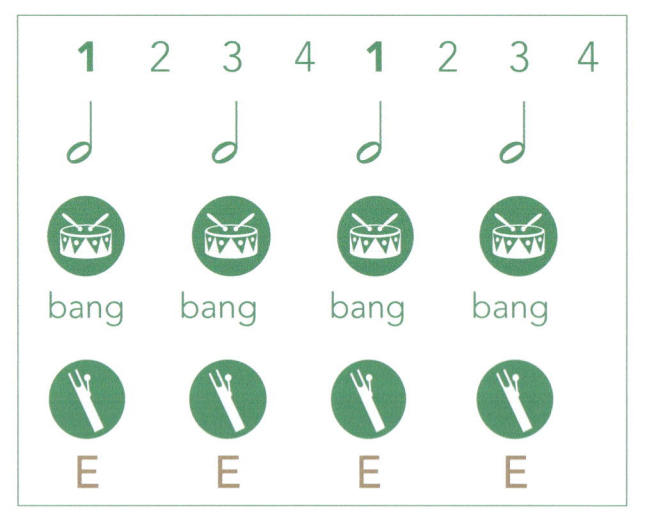

Instrumental Section 2

Introduction
Trumpet solo 1
Brass section 1
Trumpet solo 2
Brass section 2
Trumpet solo 3

drum and chime bar being played with a quicker beat

Names of notes on a keyboard

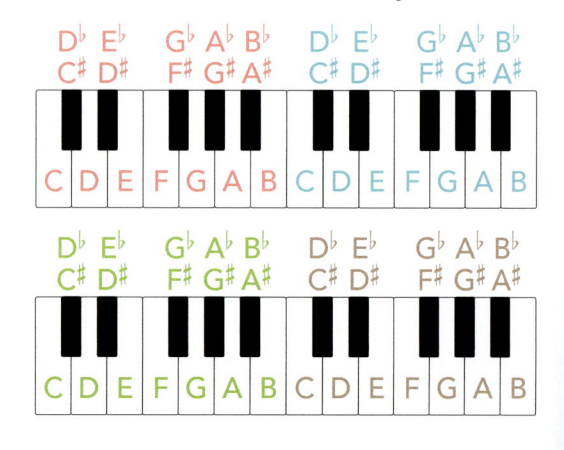

Copyright material from Ockelford, Gray, Cohen and Mai (2023), *Count Me In!*, Routledge

Soundtrack

Pattern-Makers

During the sound effects section

Show participants how to make simple patterns using pre-recorded spy movie sounds, including gun shots and evil laughter, using a switch or tablet.

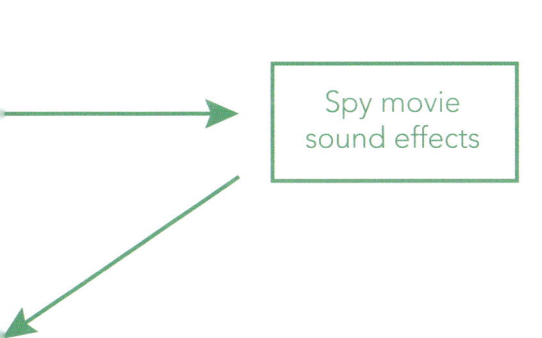

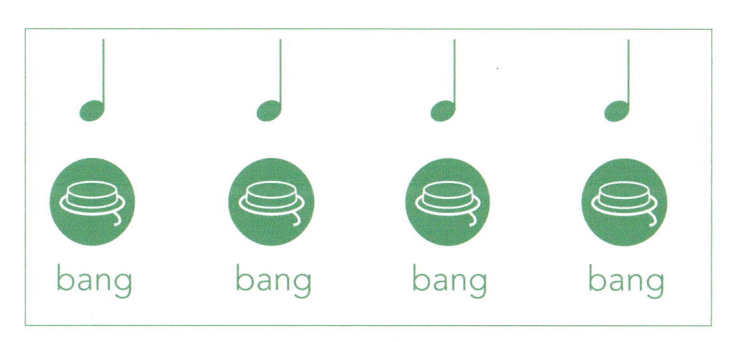

Spy movie sound effects

bang   bang   bang   bang

switch

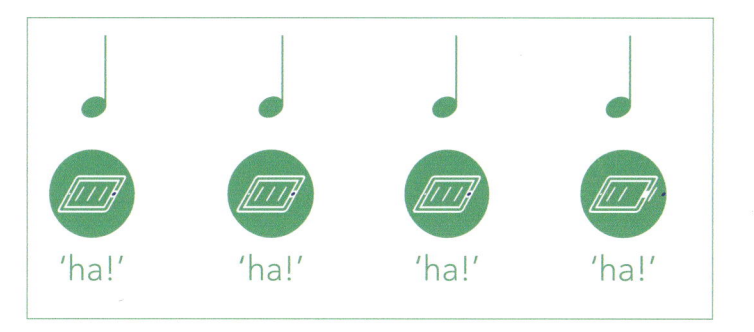

'ha!'   'ha!'   'ha!'   'ha!'

tablet

quicker repeated gunshot or laughing sounds

mic

Copyright material from Ockelford, Gray, Cohen and Mai (2023), *Count Me In!*, Routledge

Motif-Makers

During each verse

Some rhythmic, melodic and harmonic motifs are repeated through the piece. Encourage participants to practise them separately, and then join in at the right moments. There is no need to play the motifs continuously – every now and then will work well.

1	2	3	4	1	2	3	4
E		F#		G		F#	

keys

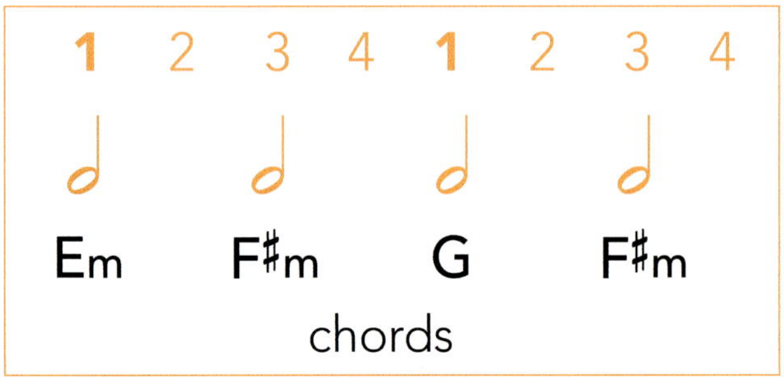

1	2	3	4	1	2	3	4
Em		F#m		G		F#m	

chords

guitar   ukulele   tablet

1	&	2	&	3	&	4	&
	E	E	E		E	E	E

bass guitar

Instrumental Section 1

Introduction
Trumpet solo 1
Brass section 1
Trumpet solo 2
Brass section 2
Trumpet solo 3

Instrumental Section 2

Introduction
Trumpet solo 1
Brass section 1
Trumpet solo 2
Brass section 2
Trumpet solo 3

Names of notes on a keyboard

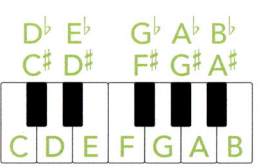

D♭ E♭   G♭ A♭ B♭
C# D#   F# G# A#
C D E F G A B

Copyright material from Ockelford, Gray, Cohen and Mai (2023), *Count Me In!*, Routledge

Soundtrack

Motif-Makers

During the sound effects section

Show participants how to connect different spy movie sounds together in various ways, choosing from digital collections of sounds triggered by keys on computers or the touch screens of tablets or phones. For example:

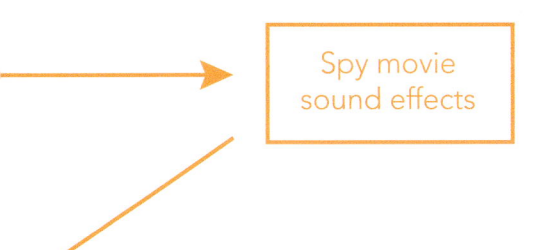

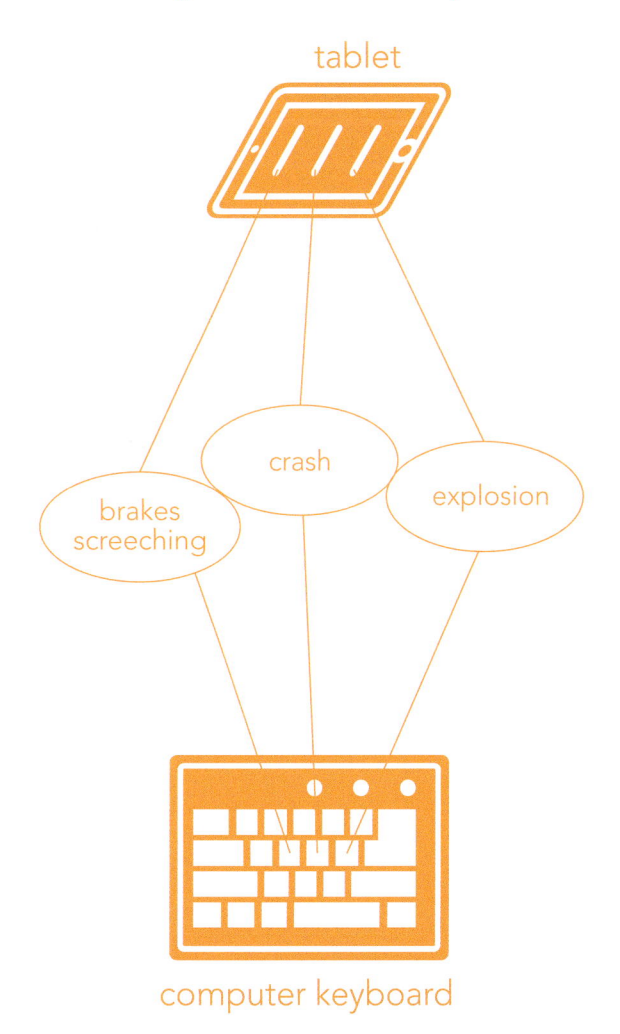

Spy movie sound effects

tablet

brakes screeching — crash — explosion

computer keyboard

Copyright material from Ockelford, Gray, Cohen and Mai (2023), *Count Me In!*, Routledge

Music-Makers

During both instrumental sections

The same four-note motif, rhythmic bass line and chords are played over and over again throughout the instrumental sections. Show participants how to play the motif on a melody instrument (such as a keyboard or recorder), and/or play the bass line on a keyboard or bass guitar. Help them to play the chords on a keyboard, guitar or ukulele, using simpler versions (in bold) if preferred.

keys   recorder   bass   guitar   ukulele

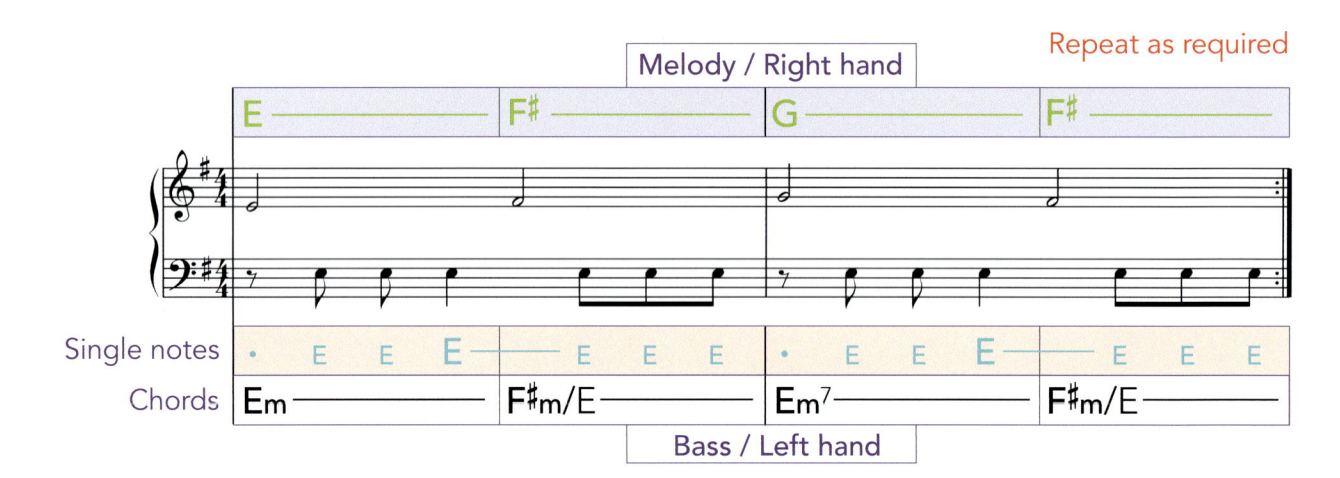

Melody / Right hand — E — F# — G — F# *Repeat as required*

Single notes: • E E E E E E E E • E E E E E E E E

Chords: Em — F#m/E — Em⁷ — F#m/E

Bass / Left hand

Teach participants to play the main tune on a melody instrument such as the keyboard.

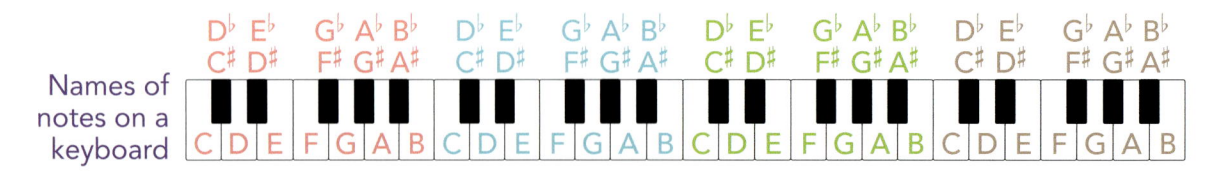

Names of notes on a keyboard:
C# D# / F# G# A# / C# D# / F# G# A# / C# D# / F# G# A# / C# D# / F# G# A#
D♭ E♭ / G♭ A♭ B♭ / D♭ E♭ / G♭ A♭ B♭ / D♭ E♭ / G♭ A♭ B♭ / D♭ E♭ / G♭ A♭ B♭
C D E F G A B / C D E F G A B / C D E F G A B / C D E F G A B

Copyright material from Ockelford, Gray, Cohen and Mai (2023), *Count Me In!*, Routledge

Soundtrack

Melody / Right hand

Score for music teachers to use

Soundtrack

Introduction

Olympic Harmony enables participants to imagine they are at the opening ceremony of the world's greatest sporting event. It opens with a fanfare on brass instruments, which sets out the first two lines of the tune. A driving drumbeat follows, then a rhythmic piano part introduces Verse 1 of the song. The tune is 'pentatonic', which means it uses only five different notes – in this case F, G, A, C and D. Various forms of pentatonic melody are common in many folk traditions, with numerous examples from Europe, the Americas, Africa and Asia. In the West, famous examples of pentatonic songs include *Amazing Grace* and *Mull of Kintyre*.

Following Verse 1, in which different parts are provided for sound-makers, pattern-makers, motif-makers and music-makers, there is a section in which all participants can improvise freely, using notes from the F, G, A, C, D pentatonic scale. It is a feature of this scale that all its notes sound moderately harmonious together, no matter how they are combined, and a pleasing effect is guaranteed.

Verse 2 is a reprise of Verse 1, followed by a final fanfare which echoes the opening of *Olympic Harmony*, and the song ends as it began, creating a symmetrical structure.

Musical resources required

Choose from the following, according to participants' abilities, preferences and needs:

Sound-Makers

- Control of digitally recorded cheering and notes from the pentatonic scale through
    - gesture recognition technology (tablets/beams)
    - eye gaze technology
    - switch(es)

  that are loaded with sound files from https://www.soundsofintent.app/count-me-in
- Microphone(s) and amplifier(s), potentially with loop pedal and effects

Pattern-Makers

- Drum(s), glockenspiel(s), chimebar(s), keyboard(s)
- Pattern-making using notes from the pentatonic scale using tablets that are loaded with sound files from https://www.soundsofintent.app/count-me-in

Motif-Makers

- Wood block(s)
- Keyboard(s), recorders(s) and/or other wind instrument(s)
- Microphone(s), amplifier(s)

Music-Makers

- Keyboard(s), recorder(s), other wind instrument(s)
- Guitar(s), ukulele(s), bass guitar(s)
- Microphone(s), amplifier(s)

Additional items

Olympic Harmony can be used to accompany a procession with a torch, flags, coloured rings and other artefacts that feature in the Olympic tradition. Each of the coloured rings could potentially be associated with one of the five pentatonic notes used in the song (perhaps by linking each with a particular chime bar or recorded muscial sound). The audience could take the part of cheering crowds to enhance the atmosphere of excitement and to help engender a feeling of togetherness.

Strategies

If possible, listen to *Olympic Harmony* for a period of time before running sessions in which participants actively engage with the music. This will help them become familiar with the sounds, patterns, motifs, melodies and harmonies that are used. Remember that in musical development – as in aural traditions – listening and observation come before people's attempts to join in.

Individual parts can be practised on a one-to-one basis, and then in pairs or in small groups, before trying to perform the piece as a whole.

During the opening fanfare, sound-makers can contribute the cheering of crowds using switches to activate digitally recorded sounds. After that, encourage pattern-makers to join in with the regular beat played on the drums, followed by motif-makers, imitating the short bursts of rhythm heard in the backing track, and finally help music-makers come in at the appropriate point with the main melody. Those facilitating the session can stimulate improvisation in the free section between verses by having a go themselves – playing any notes or motifs from the pentatonic selection F, G, A, C or D. They will all fit with the music and, whatever happens, the backing track will hold things together.

Links to other areas of experience and learning

In schools and colleges, *Olympic Harmony* has potential links to other areas of the curriculum, including physical education (sport), history (the birth of the Olympic Games and their reincarnation in modern times) and politics (how those organising the games can become embroiled in power struggles between countries).

Sound-Makers

During the fanfares

Support participants to activate digitally recorded cheering noises using switches, tablets or eye gaze technology.

switch

tablet

eye gaze

Some may be able to vocalise cheering noises, which can be made louder using a microphone and amplifier. It may be possible to add other effects, such as reverberation.

mic

Fanfare

↓

Verse 1
The world together
In sport unites,
To be a symbol
Of human rights.

Olympic harmony
Through the games resounds,
A common purpose
For all is found.

A common purpose
For all is found.

Verse 2
The world together
In sport unites,
To be a symbol
Of human rights.

Olympic harmony
Through the games resounds,
A common purpose
For all is found.

A common purpose
For all is found.

↓

Fanfare

Harmony

Sound-Makers

In the improvised section

Encourage participants to trigger individual notes from the pentatonic scale (F, A, G, C, D) using switches or eye gaze technology,

switch

eye gaze

or generate cascades of notes using beams or tablets.

beam

tablet

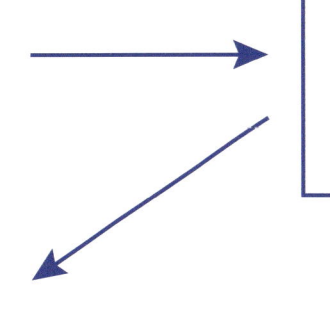

Improvised section using the pentatonic scale

Pattern-Makers

During each verse

Support participants to join in the regular beats in the song on a drum or other unpitched percussion instrument such as the tambourine.

bang · bang · bang · bang

drum

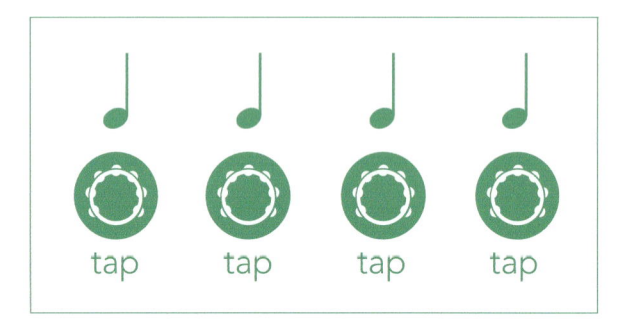

tap · tap · tap · tap

tambourine

Some participants may wish to use downloaded percussion sounds triggered by using a switch or a tablet.

switch

tablet

Fanfare
↓
Verse 1
The world together
In sport unites,
To be a symbol
Of human rights.

Olympic harmony
Through the games resounds,
A common purpose
For all is found.

A common purpose
For all is found.

Verse 2
The world together
In sport unites,
To be a symbol
Of human rights.

Olympic harmony
Through the games resounds,
A common purpose
For all is found.

A common purpose
For all is found.

↓
Fanfare

Harmony

Pattern-Makers

In the improvised section

Encourage participants to make simple patterns using notes from the pentatonic scale (F, G, A, C, D), by repeating them on melody instruments or using chime bars. For example:

```
C C C C C
F F F        G G
    D D D D
A A A A A A A A
```

Improvised section using the pentatonic scale

They may be able to make patterns of alternating notes. For example:

```
F G F G F G
D C D C
G A G A G A G A
```

- glock
- tablet
- chime bar
- keys

Names of notes on a keyboard

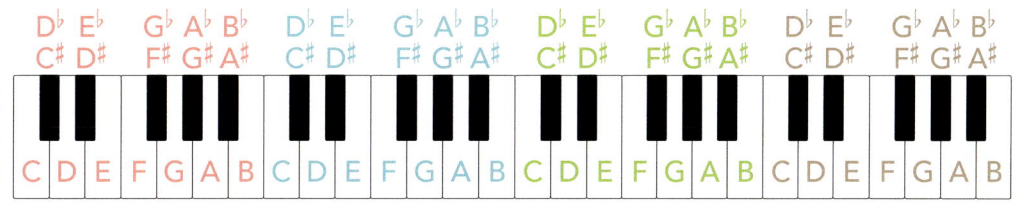

Copyright material from Ockelford, Gray, Cohen and Mai (2023), *Count Me In!*, Routledge

Motif-Makers

During each verse

Assist participants in joining in with the groove of the piece with short bursts of rhythm on a wood block or other percussion instrument. To help keep the rhythm on track, try thinking of words that fit. For example:

'now   it's   time   to   play'

wood block or drum

Some participants may wish to use downloaded percussion sounds triggered by using a switch or a tablet.

switch

tablet

Fanfare

↓

Verse 1

The world together
In sport unites,
To be a symbol
Of human rights.

Olympic harmony
Through the games resounds,
A common purpose
For all is found.

A common purpose
For all is found.

Verse 2

The world together
In sport unites,
To be a symbol
Of human rights.

Olympic harmony
Through the games resounds,
A common purpose
For all is found.

A common purpose
For all is found.

↓

Fanfare

Harmony

Motif-Makers

In the improvised section

Show participants how to make up motifs on melody instruments or by singing, using different combinations and permutations of the five notes of the pentatonic scale that is used in *Olympic Harmony* (F, G, A, C, D). These can be repeated or varied by the same player. For example:

F G C D F —

F G C D F —

F G D C F —

mic   or   keys   or   recorder

Improvised section using the pentatonic scale

Model using the motifs 'call and response' activities that fit with the backing track. For example:

CALL

F G C D F —

keys

RESPONSE

F G C D F —

keys

Names of notes on a keyboard

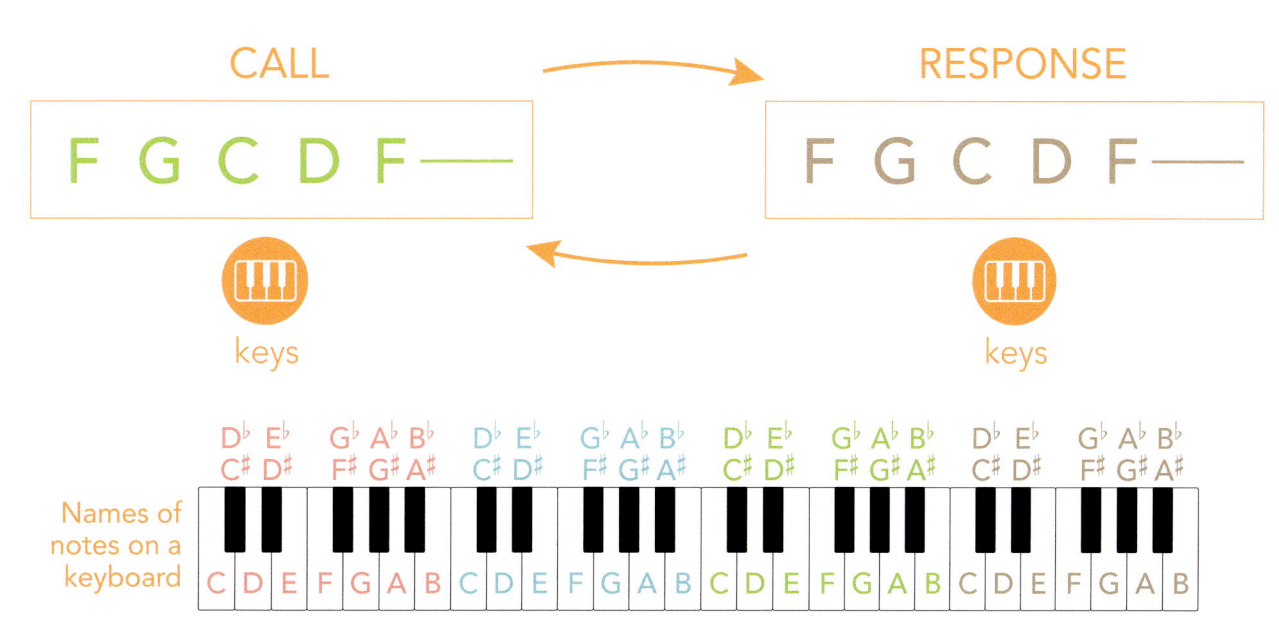

Olympic

```
┌─────────────────┐
│    Fanfare      │
└─────────────────┘
         │
         ▼
┌─────────────────────────────┐
│          Verse 1            │
│                             │
│     The world together      │
│       In sport unites,      │
│       To be a symbol        │
│       Of human rights.      │
│                             │
│      Olympic harmony        │
│   Through the games resounds,│
│      A common purpose       │
│       For all is found.     │
│                             │
│      A common purpose       │
│       For all is found.     │
└─────────────────────────────┘  ──────►  ┌─────────────────┐
                                          │   Improvised    │
                                          │  section using  │
                                          │       the       │
                                          │    pentatonic   │
                                          │      scale      │
┌─────────────────────────────┐  ◄──────  └─────────────────┘
│          Verse 2            │
│                             │
│     The world together      │
│       In sport unites,      │
│       To be a symbol        │
│       Of human rights.      │
│                             │
│      Olympic harmony        │
│   Through the games resounds,│
│      A common purpose       │
│       For all is found.     │
│                             │
│      A common purpose       │
│       For all is found.     │
└─────────────────────────────┘
         │
         ▼
┌─────────────────┐
│    Fanfare      │
└─────────────────┘
```

Copyright material from Ockelford, Gray, Cohen and Mai (2023), *Count Me In!*, Routledge

Harmony

Music-Makers

During each verse and after Verse 4

Teach participants to sing or play the tune on a melody instrument (such as a keyboard or recorder), and show them how to play the bass line on a keyboard or bass guitar. Teach them to play the chords on a keyboard, guitar or ukulele, using simpler versions (in bold) if preferred.

- mic
- keys
- recorder
- bass
- guitar
- ukulele

Right hand

Melody: G F C | C — A — | · G F D | C ——— | · G F C | C — A —

Single notes: G | A | B♭ — G | · G G G | C — G | A
Chords: Gm⁷ — | F | Gm — Gm⁷ — | Gm⁷ ——— | C⁷ — Gm⁷ — | F

Bass / Left hand

Melody: · C G—A F ——— | — A A G | A—A A — | · A A A — G | A ———

Single notes: B♭ — C — | · E♭ E♭ E♭ | F — B♭ | A | G — E♭ | — D — G
Chords: B♭⁹ — C⁷ | E♭⁹ ——— | F⁹ — B♭ | A¹³ ——— | Gm⁹ — E♭ — | D⁹ — G⁹ —

Melody: — G F C | C — A — | · C G—A | F ——————

Single notes: C — G — | A | B♭ — C | · E♭ E♭ E♭ | F
Chords: C — Gm⁷ — | F | B♭⁹ — C⁷ | E♭⁹ ——— | F⁹

Names of notes on a keyboard

Copyright material from Ockelford, Gray, Cohen and Mai (2023), *Count Me In!*, Routledge

Olympi

Score for music teachers to use

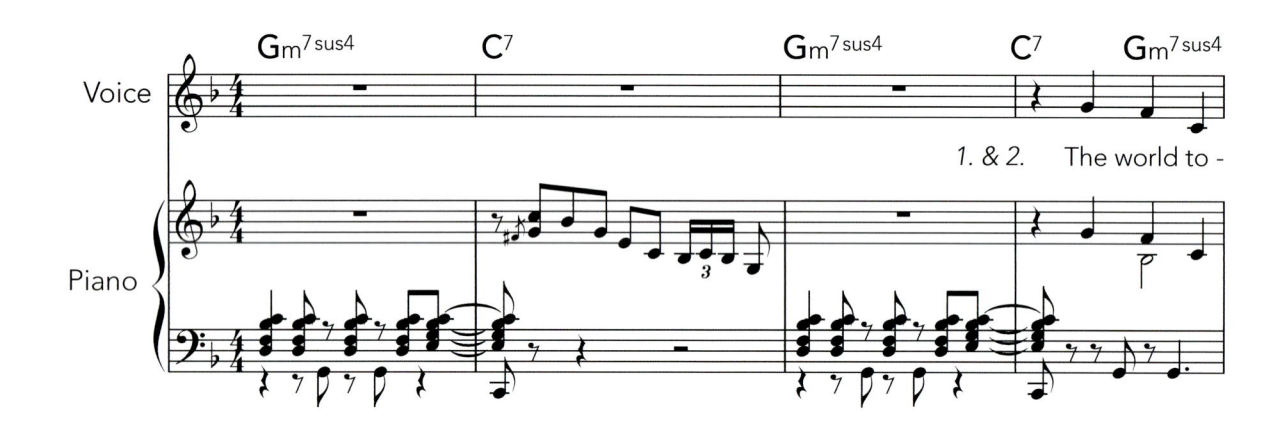

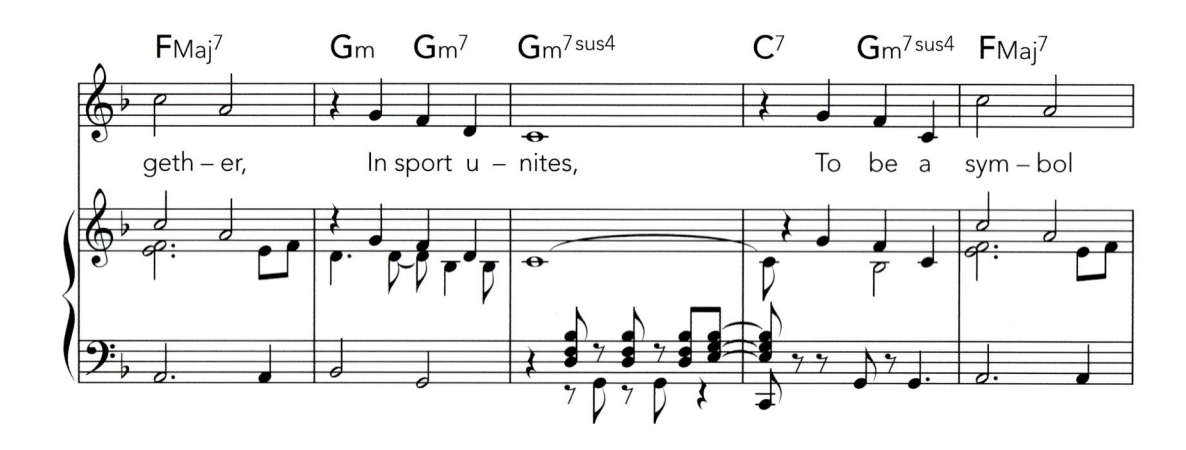

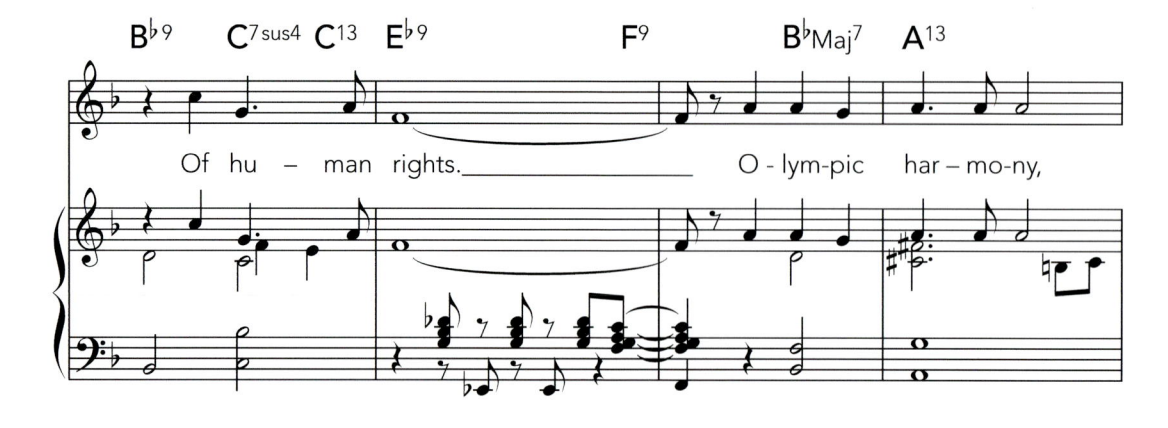

1. & 2. The world to-geth – er, In sport u – nites, To be a sym – bol Of hu – man rights._____ O - lym-pic har – mo-ny,

Harmony

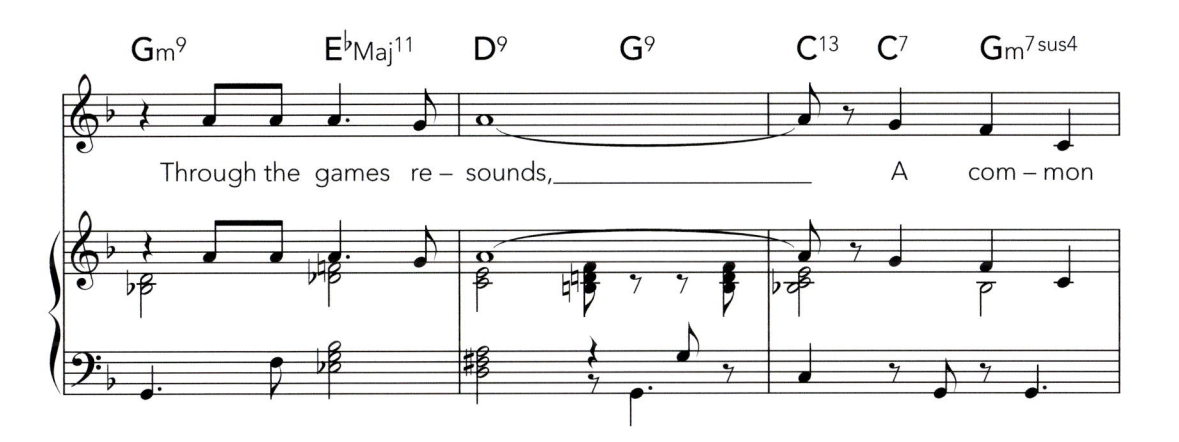

Through the games re – sounds,_____ A com – mon pur – pose For all is found._____

Introduction

Computer Chip Rock is written in the style of mid-1950s rock 'n' roll, a form of music that originated from African-American genres such as gospel, jazz, boogie-woogie, and rhythm and blues. The song uses the three chords characteristic of the style (I, IV and V), with 'blues' notes appearing prominently in the melody (A flat and E flat). Rhythmically, groups of three notes ('triplets') keep the music moving forward, while the rock 'n' roll feel is strengthened by the 'backbeats' (on the counts of 2 and 4) on the snare drum.

Computer Chip Rock is designed to be fun to play and sing, fusing a mid-twentieth-century style of popular music with lyrics that address a contemporary issue: our day-to-day reliance on computer chips.

There are distinct parts for sound-makers, pattern-makers, motif-makers and music-makers, so everyone, irrespective of their musical abilities, can join in. At the end of each verse, participants can choose an item of technology using a range of downloadable digital sounds.

Musical resources required

Choose from the following according to participants' abilities, preferences and needs:

Sound-Makers

- Wrist bells
- Control of digitally recorded sounds from TVs through
    - gesture recognition technology (tablets/beams)
    - eye gaze technology
    - switch(es)

  that are loaded with sound files from https://www.soundsofintent.app/count-me-in
- Microphone(s) and amplifier(s), potentially with loop pedal and effects

Pattern-Makers

- Wood block(s), drum(s),
- Pattern-making through individually recorded ringtones using a switch or switches that are loaded with sound files from https://www.soundsofintent.app/count-me-in

Motif-Makers

- Tambourine(s)
- Keyboard(s)

Chip Rock

- Computer(s) and/or tablet(s), loaded with a selection of car sounds
- Microphone(s), amplifier(s)

Music-Makers

- Keyboard(s), recorder(s) and/or other wind instrument(s)
- Guitar(s), ukulele(s), bass guitar(s)
- Computer(s) and/or tablet(s) with software to create a soundscape using game sounds, downloaded from https://www.soundsofintent.app/count-me-in
- Microphone(s), amplifier(s)

Additional items

Computer Chip Rock can be performed in combination with a series of pictures or video excerpts showing everyday items of technology in action. It could involve participants making dance moves in the style of 1950s rock 'n' roll, perhaps dressed in clothes or accessories in the style of that era.

Strategies

Play *Computer Chip Rock* to participants several times over a few days before encouraging them to have a go themselves, enabling them to become familiar with the sounds, patterns, motifs, melodies and harmonies that are used in the song. This is in accord with the principle that, in children's musical development – as in aural traditions – listening precedes active participation.

Practise individual parts with participants on their own, and then in pairs or small groups, before bringing everyone together.

Using the backing track, start each verse with sound-makers, then introduce pattern-makers and motif-makers, before music-makers enter with the main melody. The arrangements are designed to suit all participants, whatever their level of musical development. If some people are absent on a particular occasion, or if their concentration should fluctuate when it is their turn to play or sing, the backing track will ensure the flow of the music is maintained.

Links to other areas of experience and learning

In schools and colleges, *Computer Chip Rock* has potential links to other curricular areas, such as information technology and the history of popular Western culture in the 1950s.

Computer

Sound-Makers

During each verse

Support participants to shake wrist bells or ankle bells from time to time.

wrist bells

Help them make similar sounds by activating digitally recorded jingly bell sounds using gesture recognition technology such as that available on tablets and using beams,

tablet

beam

or by using switches or eye gaze technology.

switch

eye gaze

Verse 1
Whatever you got,
If you use it a lot,
Washing machine or TV screen,
It needs a chip
To be equipped.
Whatever the kit,
There's always a chip to fit.

Verse 2
Whatever you got,
If you use it a lot,
Computer or phone or tablet or drone,
It needs a chip
To be equipped.
Whatever the kit,
There's always a chip to fit.

Verse 3
Whatever you got,
If you use it a lot,
Car or van or train or plane,
It needs a chip
To be equipped.
Whatever the kit,
There's always a chip to fit.

Verse 4
Whatever you got,
If you use it a lot,
Oven or hob or car key fob,
It needs a chip
To be equipped.
Whatever the kit,
There's always a chip to fit.

Copyright material from Ockelford, Gray, Cohen and Mai (2023), *Count Me In!*, Routledge

Chip Rock

What have you got?
That you use a lot?
I've got a TV.
I've got a TV.
Listen to me, you'll hear
I've got a TV.

What have you got?
That you use a lot?
I've got a phone.
I've got a phone.
Listen to me, you'll hear
I've got a phone.

What have you got?
That you use a lot?
We've got a car.
We've got a car
Listen to me, you'll hear
We've got a car..

What have you got?
That you use a lot?
I've got a game.
I've got a game
Listen to me, you'll hear
I've got a game..

Sound-Makers

After Verse 1

Enable participants to trigger pre-recorded or downloaded digital TV sounds using a switch, a tablet or eye gaze technology.

switch eye gaze tablet

Different options can be presented and used to provide a context for choosing and to express preferences.

Alternatively, participants may make sounds using their voices, which can be made louder using a microphone and amplifier, with the possibility of adding effects and looping.

mic

It may the that the vocal sound that a participant makes naturally is similar to that produced by an everyday item of technology, in which case that connection can be used in the song. For example, a whirring sound may sound a bit like a food mixer. While the participant concerned may be unaware of the link that is made, others may understand it, and, provided the act of appropriation is done respectfully, it may well help to promote a sense of group belonging.

Copyright material from Ockelford, Gray, Cohen and Mai (2023), *Count Me In!*, Routledge

Compute

Pattern-Makers

During each verse

Encourage participants to join in the regular beat of the song on an instrument such as the wood block. The drum is 'on the beat', and the wood block is 'off the beat'. It can be difficult to play off the beat to start with, and it may help to play the instruments alternately: left hand, right hand, and so on.

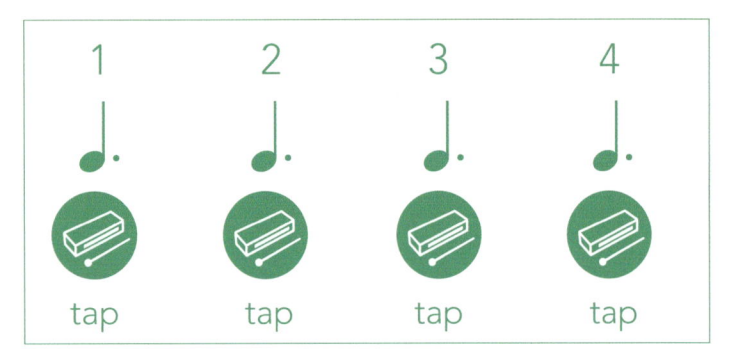

1	2	3	4
tap	tap	tap	tap

wood block

Next, help participants to play along with the snare drum in the recording, which sounds on beats 2 and 4 in each bar.

1	**2**	3	**4**
	bang		bang

drum

Make digitally recorded sounds available to play using a switch or a tablet.

switch · tablet

Verse 1
Whatever you got,
If you use it a lot,
Washing machine or TV screen,
It needs a chip
To be equipped.
Whatever the kit,
There's always a chip to fit.

↓

Verse 2
Whatever you got,
If you use it a lot,
Computer or phone or tablet or drone,
It needs a chip
To be equipped.
Whatever the kit,
There's always a chip to fit.

↓

Verse 3
Whatever you got,
If you use it a lot,
Car or van or train or plane,
It needs a chip
To be equipped.
Whatever the kit,
There's always a chip to fit.

↓

Verse 4
Whatever you got,
If you use it a lot,
Oven or hob or car key fob,
It needs a chip
To be equipped.
Whatever the kit,
There's always a chip to fit.

Copyright material from Ockelford, Gray, Cohen and Mai (2023), *Count Me In!*, Routledge

Chip Rock

Pattern-Makers

After Verse 2

Show participants how to use digitally downloaded sounds of a phone ringing to create simple patterns, by repeating them using a switch or touchscreen on a tablet.

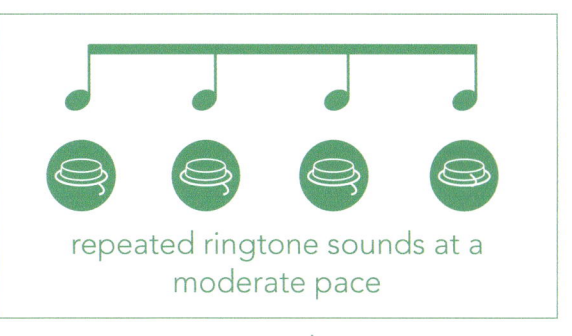

What have you got?
That you use a lot?
I've got a TV.
I've got a TV.
Listen to me, you'll hear
I've got a TV.

repeated ringtone sounds at a moderate pace

switch

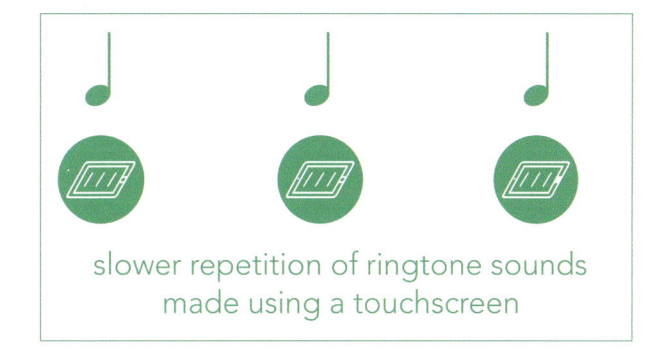

What have you got?
That you use a lot?
I've got a phone.
I've got a phone.
Listen to me, you'll hear
I've got a phone.

slower repetition of ringtone sounds made using a touchscreen

tablet

What have you got?
That you use a lot?
We've got a car.
We've got a car.
Listen to me, you'll hear
We've got a car.

Some participants may enjoy making ringtone sounds vocally, and enhancing them with a microphone and amplifier.

What have you got?
That you use a lot?
I've got a game.
I've got a game.
Listen to me, you'll hear
I've got a game.

quicker ringtone sounds made vocally

mic

Copyright material from Ockelford, Gray, Cohen and Mai (2023), *Count Me In!*, Routledge

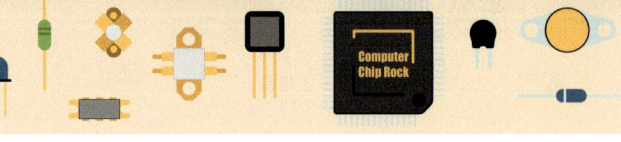

Compute

Motif-Makers

During each verse

Demonstrate how to join in with the groove of the piece with short bursts of rhythm on a tambourine. It may help to think of a phrase that fits. For example:

'com – pu – ter chip'

tambourine

Model joining in with the first line of each verse, singing and/or playing.

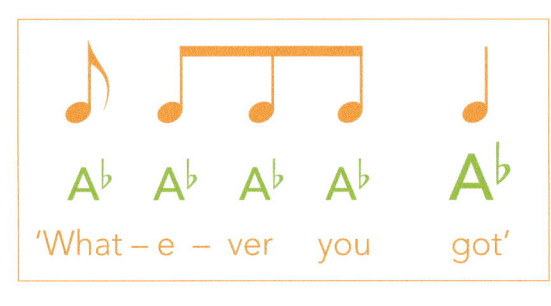

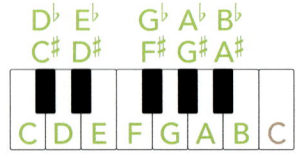

A♭ A♭ A♭ A♭ A♭
'What – e – ver you got'

mic   keys

D♭ E♭   G♭ A♭ B♭
C# D#   F# G# A#

C D E F G A B C

Names of notes on a keyboard

Verse 1
Whatever you got,
If you use it a lot,
Washing machine or TV screen,
It needs a chip
To be equipped.
Whatever the kit,
There's always a chip to fit.

Verse 2
Whatever you got,
If you use it a lot,
Computer or phone or tablet or drone,
It needs a chip
To be equipped.
Whatever the kit,
There's always a chip to fit.

Verse 3
Whatever you got,
If you use it a lot,
Car or van or train or plane,
It needs a chip
To be equipped.
Whatever the kit,
There's always a chip to fit.

Verse 4
Whatever you got,
If you use it a lot,
Oven or hob or car key fob,
It needs a chip
To be equipped.
Whatever the kit,
There's always a chip to fit.

Copyright material from Ockelford, Gray, Cohen and Mai (2023), *Count Me In!*, Routledge

Chip Rock

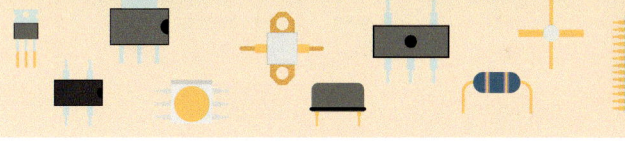

Motif-Makers
After Verse 3

Show participants how to connect together different groups of digitally recorded sounds such as the ringtones of phones or the different start-up sounds of computers, choosing from collections of sounds triggered by keys on computers or the touch screens of tablets or phones.

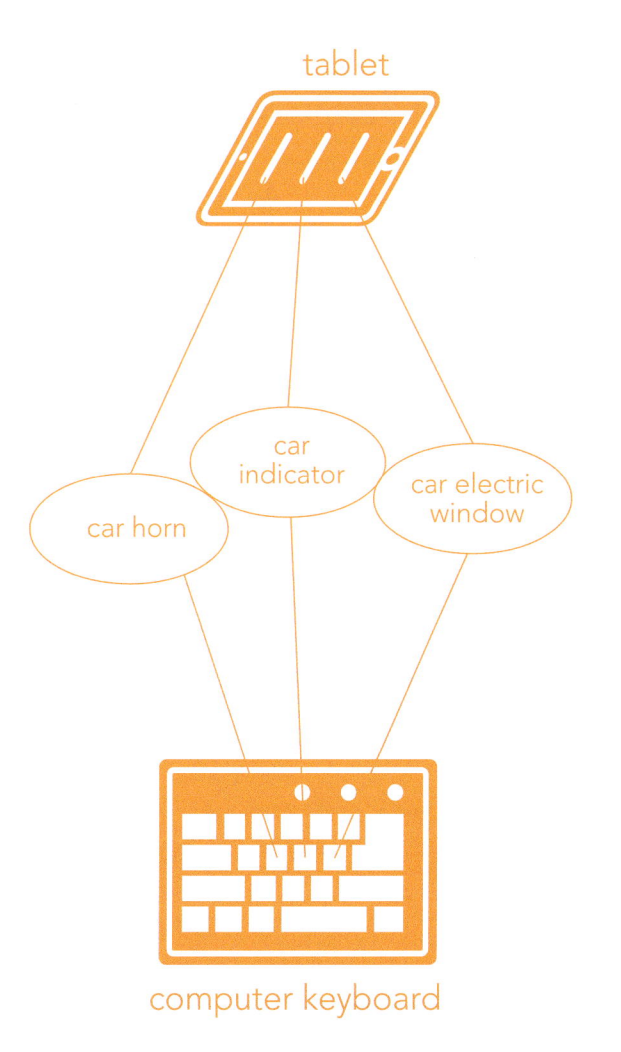

What have you got?
That you use a lot?
I've got a TV.
I've got a TV.
Listen to me, you'll hear
I've got a TV.

What have you got?
That you use a lot?
I've got a phone.
I've got a phone.
Listen to me, you'll hear
I've got a phone.

What have you got?
That you use a lot?
We've got a car.
We've got a car.
Listen to me, you'll hear
We've got a car.

What have you got?
That you use a lot?
I've got a game.
I've got a game.
Listen to me, you'll hear
I've got a game.

tablet

car horn — car indicator — car electric window

computer keyboard

Computer Chip Rock

Verse 1
Whatever you got,
If you use it a lot,
Washing machine or TV screen,
It needs a chip
To be equipped.
Whatever the kit,
There's always a chip to fit.

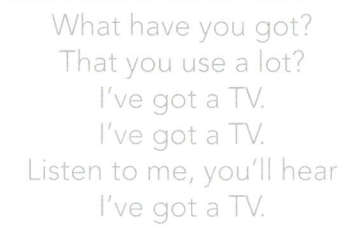

> What have you got?
> That you use a lot?
> I've got a TV.
> I've got a TV.
> Listen to me, you'll hear
> I've got a TV.

Verse 2
Whatever you got,
If you use it a lot,
Computer or phone or tablet or drone,
It needs a chip
To be equipped.
Whatever the kit,
There's always a chip to fit.

> What have you got?
> That you use a lot?
> I've got a phone.
> I've got a phone.
> Listen to me, you'll hear
> I've got a phone.

Verse 3
Whatever you got,
If you use it a lot,
Car or van or train or plane,
It needs a chip
To be equipped.
Whatever the kit,
There's always a chip to fit.

> What have you got?
> That you use a lot?
> We've got a car.
> We've got a car.
> Listen to me, you'll hear
> We've got a car.

Verse 4
Whatever you got,
If you use it a lot,
Oven or hob or car key fob,
It needs a chip
To be equipped.
Whatever the kit,
There's always a chip to fit.

> What have you got?
> That you use a lot?
> I've got a game.
> I've got a game.
> Listen to me, you'll hear
> I've got a game.

Chip Rock

Music-Makers

After Verse 4

Before a performance of *Computer Chip Rock*, help participants to create a short soundscape of digitally recorded sounds made by technological devices using an app such as GarageBand. Replay the montage of sounds after Verse 4.

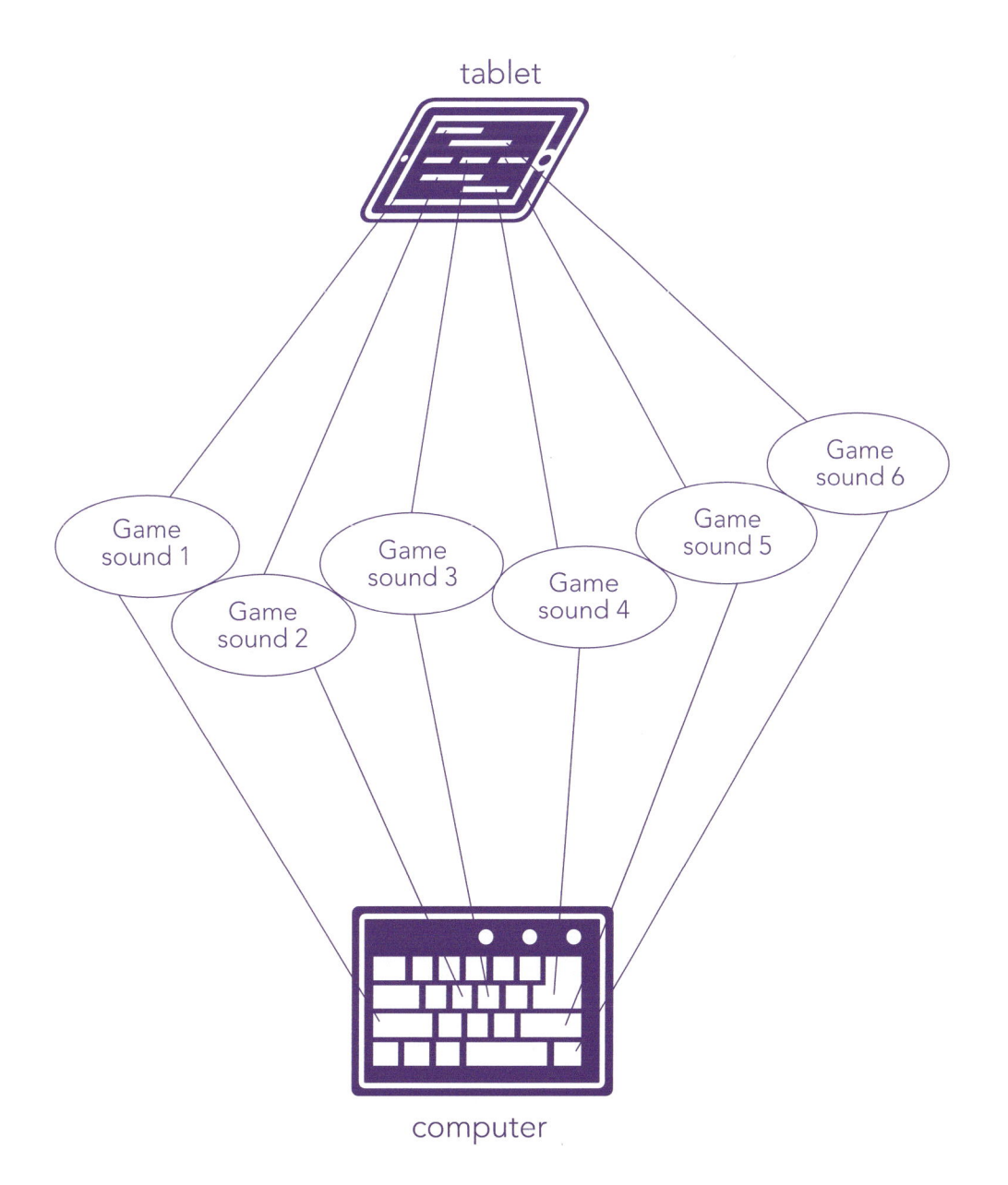

tablet

- Game sound 1
- Game sound 2
- Game sound 3
- Game sound 4
- Game sound 5
- Game sound 6

computer

Copyright material from Ockelford, Gray, Cohen and Mai (2023), *Count Me In!*, Routledge

Computer Chip Rock

Music-Makers

During each verse

Teach participants to sing or play the tune on a melody instrument (such as a keyboard or recorder), or to play the bass line on a keyboard or bass guitar. They may also learn the chords on a keyboard, guitar or ukulele, using simpler versions (in bold) if preferred.

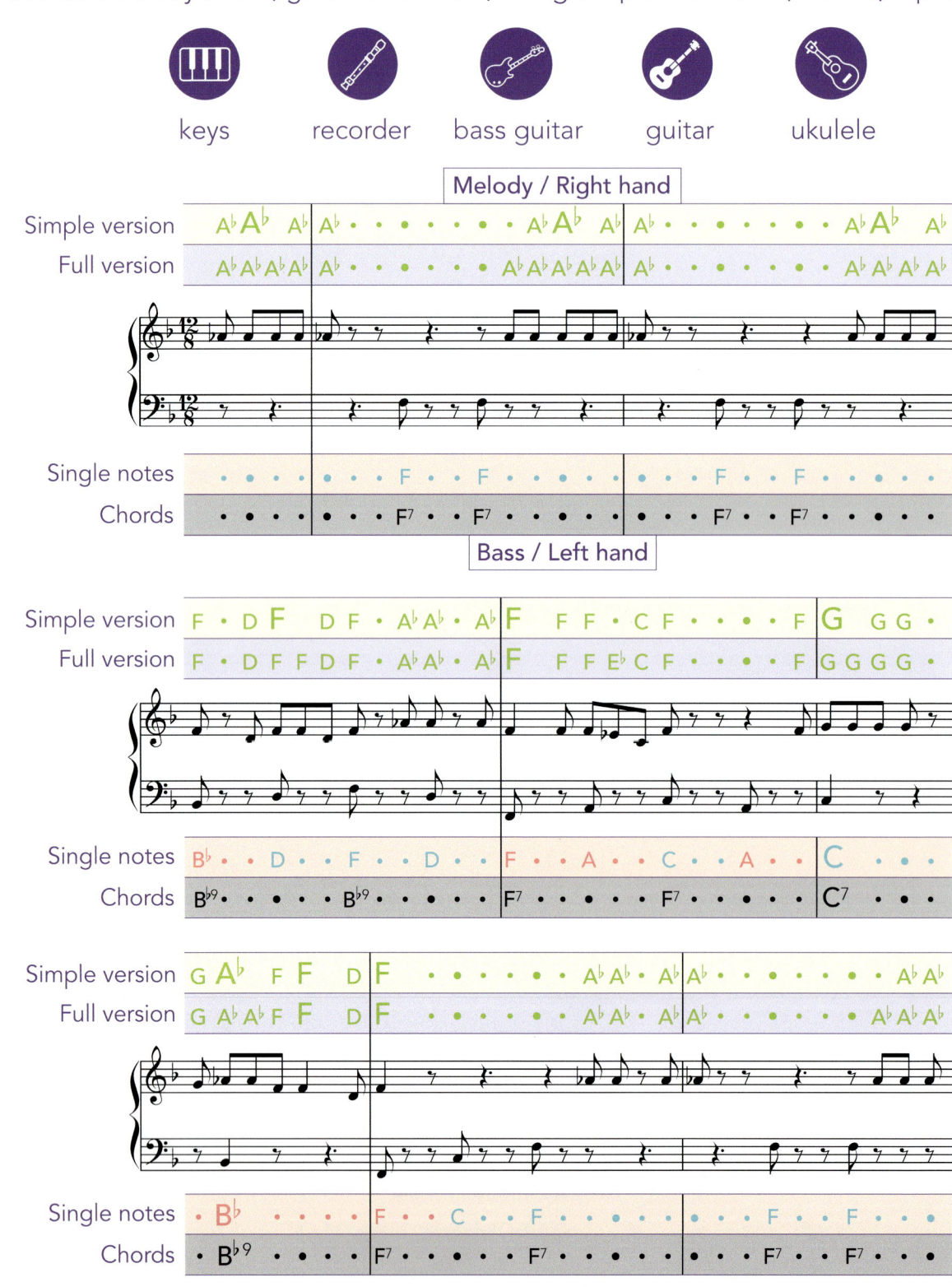

- keys
- recorder
- bass guitar
- guitar
- ukulele

Melody / Right hand

Simple version	A♭ A♭ A♭ · · · · · · A♭ A♭ A♭	A♭ · · · · · · A♭ A♭ A♭
Full version	A♭ A♭ A♭ A♭ · · · · · A♭ A♭ A♭ A♭	A♭ · · · · · · A♭ A♭ A♭

| Single notes | · · · · · F · · F · · · · · · F · · F · · · |
| Chords | · · · · F⁷ · · F⁷ · · · · · F⁷ · · F⁷ · · · |

Bass / Left hand

| Simple version | F · D F   D F · A♭ A♭ · A♭ | F   F F · C F · · · · F | G   G G · |
| Full version | F · D F F D F · A♭ A♭ · A♭ | F   F F E♭ C F · · · F | G G G G · |

| Single notes | B♭ · D · · F · D · · F · A · · C · · A · · C · · |
| Chords | B♭♭⁹ · · · B♭♭⁹ · · · · F⁷ · · · F⁷ · · · C⁷ · · · |

| Simple version | G A♭   F F   D F · · · · · A♭ A♭ · A♭ A♭ · · · · A♭ A♭ |
| Full version | G A♭ A♭ F F   D F · · · · A♭ A♭ · A♭ A♭ · · · A♭ A♭ A♭ |

| Single notes | · B♭ · · · · · · F · · C · F · · · · · · F · · F · · · |
| Chords | · B♭♭⁹ · · · · · F⁷ · · · · F⁷ · · · · · · F⁷ · · F⁷ · · · |

Copyright material from Ockelford, Gray, Cohen and Mai (2023), *Count Me In!*, Routledge

Chip Rock

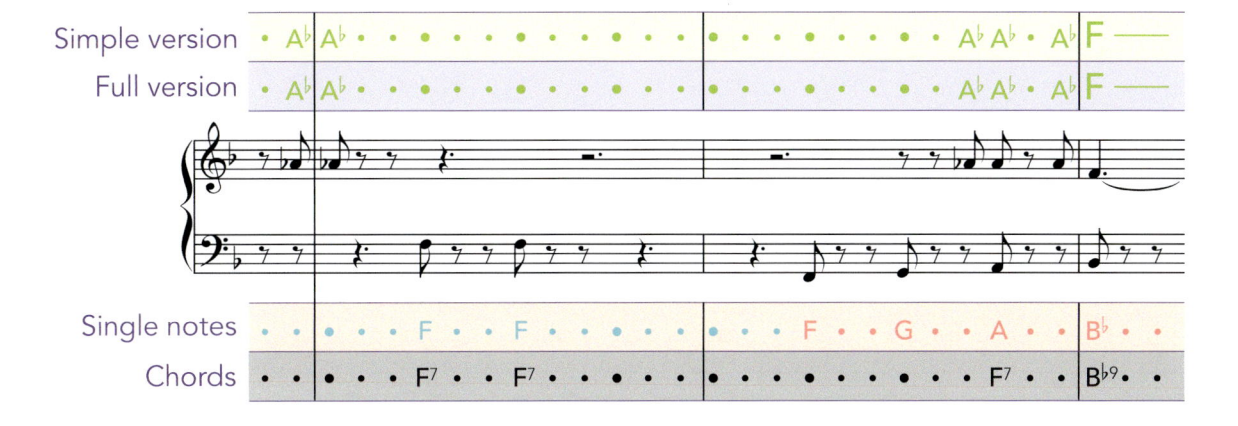

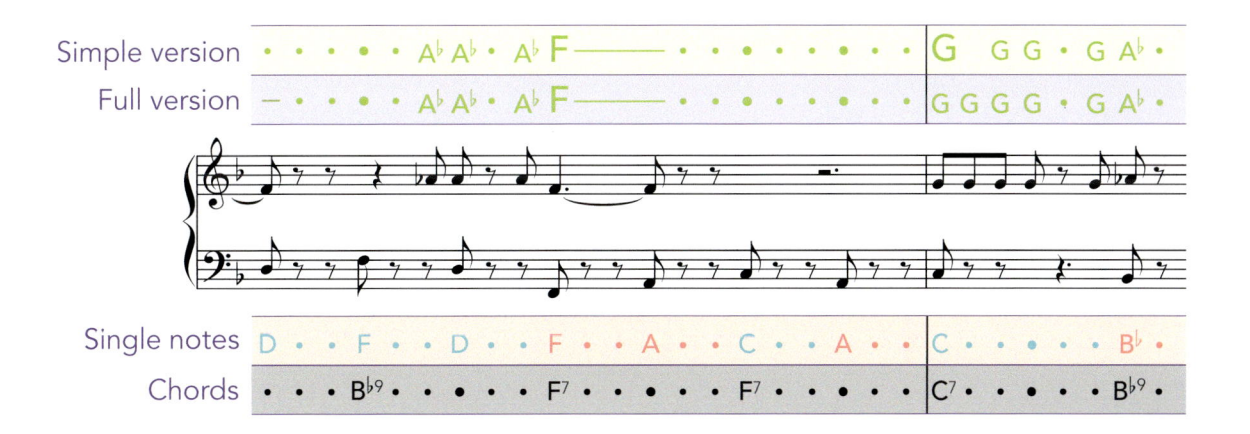

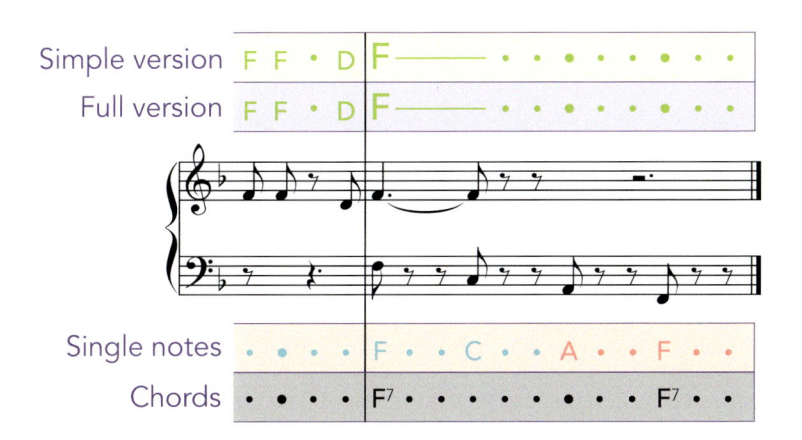

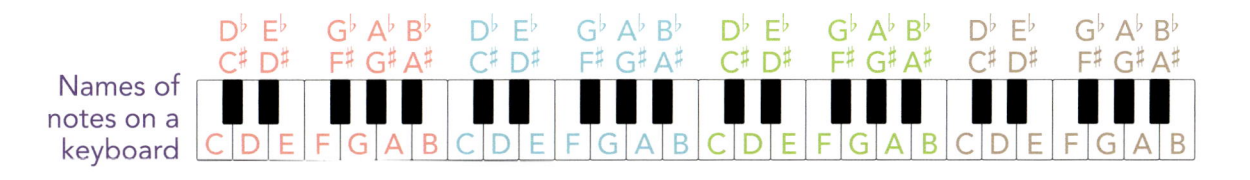

Compute

Score for music teachers to use

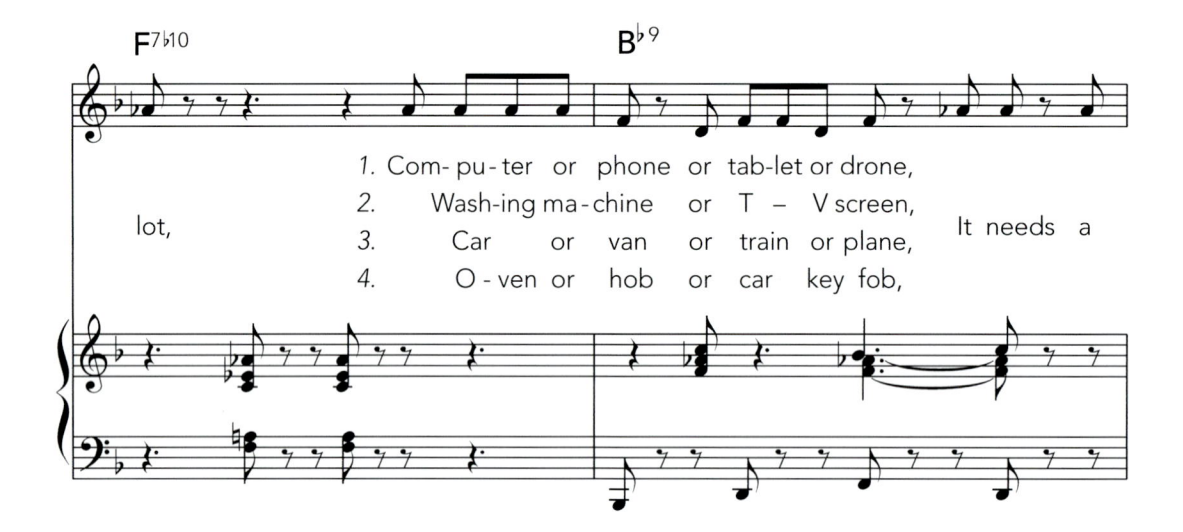

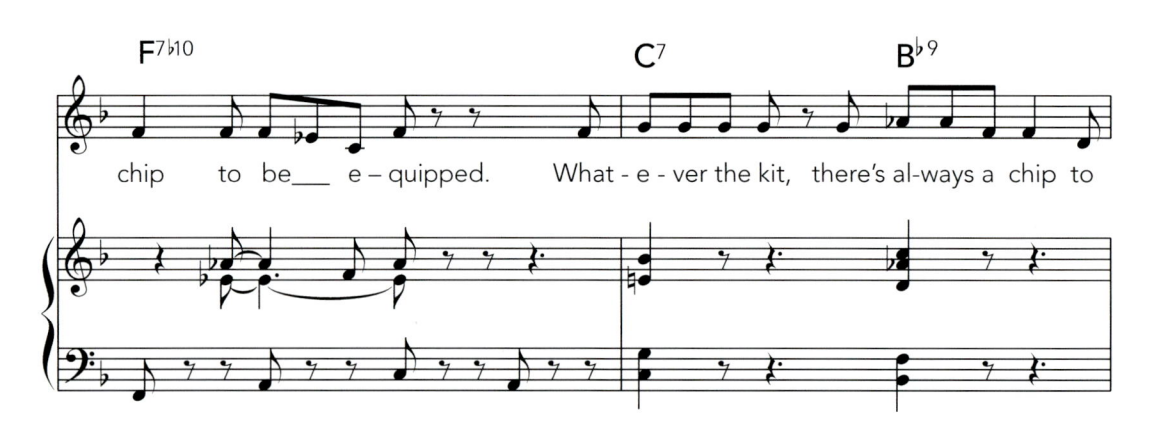

Chip Rock

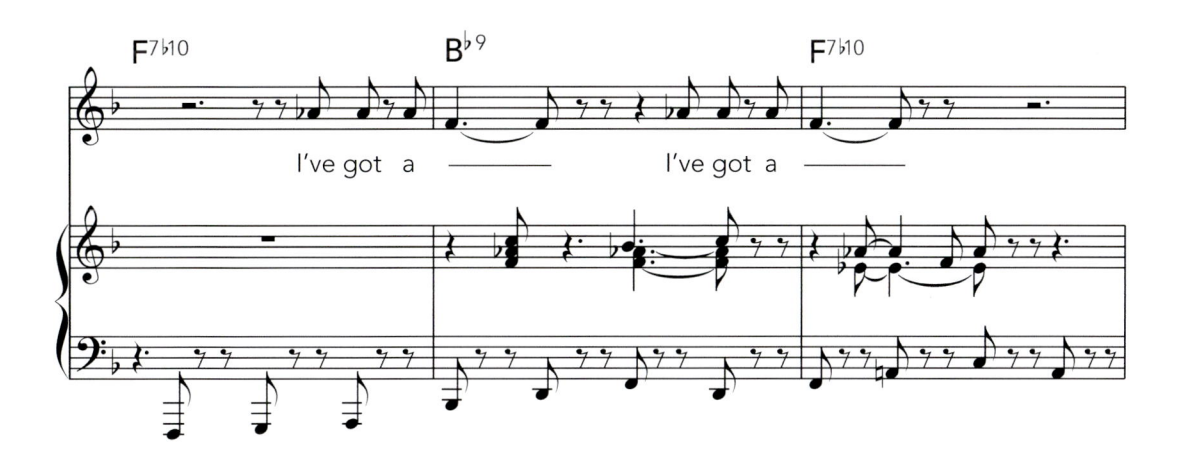

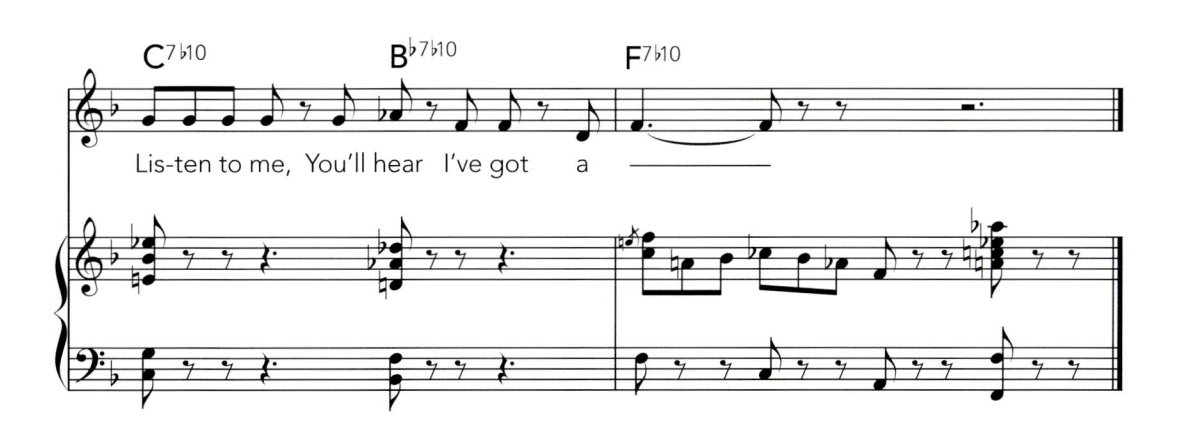